WRITE, BELOVED, WRITE

The Living-Breathing Poetry of God

by

marybeth and Jesus

Come to Me.
Reach for Me.
Love Me.
Seek More of Me.
He beseeches,
Share Me.
Speak of Our alchemy.
Open your heart
to My Living Word,
My Reality and
Write of Me...

Printed in the United States of America

First Printing, 2019

ISBN: 978-1-54396-696-1

Cover by Nancy O. Schirmer

CONTENTS

FOREWORD

It was a snowy, rainy weekend in March, 2006 that I met MaryBeth. She was leading a retreat in New Hampshire with 75 attendees. What struck me that opening night was the way she walked to the podium, big boots untied, flopping against the chapel floor. I was impressed with her unpretentiousness, which made me laugh. The woman next to me whispered, *There's MaryBeth. She's such a saint.* I thought, *Let's see how much of a saint she is after a few hours with me!*

This marked the beginning of a thirteen year relationship of working together to know Jesus and live His Plan. We have engaged in thousands of spiritual conversations, sat in meditation hundreds of times and co-facilitated nearly one hundred retreats. There are more than four hundred miles between our homes, yet our devotion could not be dampened. We embarked on a spiritual adventure, deepening in intimate relationship with Jesus.

Over the years my understanding of our shared purpose grew and gathered Light. MaryBeth has a gift for hearing the Voice for Love. I have also been eager to hear. It is my grand desire to fulfill the Will of God. How can I do so if I don't hear His Voice?

Our every visit involved meditation, opening the heart and practicing lessons of *A Course in Miracles*. I am often prompted to ask what messages Spirit would share, sometimes pertaining to an individual situation, always encompassing a universal application. I cherish hearing His Voice, seeing through His Eyes and feeling His Love. The years have brought a growing realization of the Christ within me and a deepening of communication, an effect of MaryBeth's demonstration.

During our visits we would enter into quiet contemplation. Within a short time the meditation would be interrupted. MaryBeth would grab her pen writing rapidly with fixed and devoted attention. Jess (her affectionate nickname for Jesus) poured through. We would return to silence for a brief period, and again she would reach for the pen scribing intently, ardently. Sharing our inner experiences, communications and understandings, we grew open and accepting of the Voice for Love.

A significant aspect of my role in this process was affirmation. Many times I would ask, *Will you read the message you heard?* MaryBeth would shrink back saying, *I don't know if this is any good. I'm not sure of this. It doesn't sound right to me.* She was concerned that the communication be pure and true. Along with Jess, she was aware of a false inner-loper, a judge within rejecting the writings and her *Self.* Each time she read, I was moved. Not only was there depth and wholeness of thought but it came through as exquisite, beautiful poetry. It came through as *Answer.*

I am not alone in recognizing the value of these conversations. Participants at our gatherings and retreats are astonished by the outpouring of poetry. It is uplifting and personally validating to see others touched as I have been.

Long-time members of the Foundation of Open Hearts have healed and grown through exploration of these scribings coupled with the loving presence of MaryBeth. We continue to offer retreats and sessions for those who thirst to know the Love of Jesus and follow His Wisdom.

I feel privileged for the part given me as I journey more intimately together with Jess and MaryBeth. It has been a discipline of listening, obeying, and healing. It continues to be a celebration of the Reality of a Supreme and Loving Brother.

I trust that *Write, Beloved, Write* will touch your heart as you explore this powerful book. Perhaps you will glimpse your own life as a Living-Breathing Poem of God.

Richard Dignan

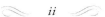

UNRAVELING
THE LANGUAGE FOR
UNDERSTANDING
THIS BOOK

Jess, or Jesse is Jesus, or sometimes called Jeshua.

Lily is the name Jess has given me.

You will also see my name written as marybeth. I forego the use of capitals purposely.

Capitals are for God. You will see many words written in capitals that normally do not call for capitalization. These words reflect God attributes, virtues, personality.

Grandpoppi or sometimes Grand Papa is the name of Our Father, Creator.

ACIM is the abbreviation for *A Course In Miracles*, a three volume work scribed by Helen Schucman and Bill Thetford. It is also called, *The Course.* I have been a student and teacher of its poetry and healing message for nearly thirty years. There are many editions of the book. The two that I use most often in this work are:

> Original Edition published by Course in Miracles Society. Quotes are cited Or.E. preceding the chapters and paragraphs;

> Foundation for Inner Peace, edited version. Quotes are cited ACIM preceding the chapters and paragraphs.

FINAL PREFACE!

Like all things about these writings, the opening words do not seem to me to belong together, but this is His humor and the nature of the book itself. I have tried for days to write an opening to this book, scribbling pages in an attempt to capture the conversations within. The words are deficient. Frustrated and weary I went to the couch (my meditation) straight from rising. I heard His Voice, *Good morning*. It was a cheery and welcoming sound that set me immediately to crying. Perhaps I thought He had gone.

(Jess)
You have a lot of things to say about Me, a lot of descriptions.

(marybeth)
Yes, I want to write a proper introduction to this book but I have been blocked for days.
Where have you been?

(Jess)
I am in the end,
just as I am in
the beginning,
The First and the Last.
I never leave you.
I never betray you.
My Word is true
today, yesterday;
limitless, unbound,
beyond days as you

count them,
and of course,
I am here, now,
beyond fear
(which has numbered
the words of this
introduction),
My Heart an
eternal Home for
the living-breathing
poem of You.

(marybeth)
I have been afraid to end this book. I feel loss, and also doubt.
Will there be repercussions from admitting that I hear You,
that I have walked with You this way? I am like Simon Peter
who denied he loved You, thrice, believing association with You
will lead to persecution.
I persecute my *Self.*

(Jess)
Remember then
what I said to Simon
as I implore you again,
Do you love Me?
Then feed my lambs.
Do you love Me?
Then feed my sheep
Do you love Me? (John 21:17)
This is not a bit of straw
we offer the world.
Love Me with your

whole heart and
give everything
that Love may be
complete,
as I give you My *Self,*
as I Love you
completely.

Loving Me fulfills
the Law of Grandpoppi *
that the channels of Creation
be opened
through Association
and Holy Relationship with Me.
Together, we are the Way,
the Truth, and the Light
in this World.
We are the Living-Breathing
Poem of God.
We are *together* The Voice
that cries out
in the wilderness,
and the Word that heals
the parched heart.
We are One
and this Union
has but begun,
reborn each time you
come to Me.

*Grandpoppi is the nickname of Our Father, Creator.

Come to Me
holy emptied of your
books, your explanations,
your doubts.

Understand,
these pages are not given
to work in the world.
It is given to you,
a gift of Truth,
that you might share
and come to know
your Self.
Knowing your Self
as I do, you will see
it is easy to Love You.

I tell you again,
the end is in the beginning
and the beginning, the end:
the end
of the world of lovelessness,
of laws and fears you made
to block Love's Presence,
to shut the Light and say
goodnight to these writings.

Like our Holy Relationship
they are only now
expanding and seeding
your awareness with
My Reality,
only NOW,

turning the page
in your mind
from past dirges
to the Song of Salvation,
a Song Solomon sang,
as God knocked upon
the door of creation
seeking welcome in
human Hearts,
seeking Presence
in hearts shut tight
to His Devotion.

So here am I
to write My Self
and give you permission
to refrain from
descriptions that make
attempts to pen
an enticing entrance
for God.

The beginning is not here
but in Our Great Grandpoppi
Who approves of this message
as I do approve
and covet You,
Our Voice for Love
and Beloved of God.

Do not fear that I will
here-in, leave you.
I come again

in patience and joy
to share the womb
you have prepared for Me.
I knock upon the door
persistently,
until you leave
the entry open,
when We need not wait
longer
to scribe the Light,
to Live the Poem,
to Breathe the One Breath
of the Son of Source,
of The Word
become flesh;
the true beginning
of Our story here,
the Author who
We love to credit.

Let the summit
and the valley,
the journey's dawn
and dimming dusk
praise Him,
glorify His ineffable
Book of Life,
His Omniscience
and Love for Human Being
Which cannot be described
neither written
but shines behind

these letters
and gives them Life.
He is the Creator
of the Living-Breathing Poem,
the Word scribed in Light,
the Alpha and Omega,
within and between all lines,
unwritten as Law,
and bound tight in Volumes
we do not yet understand,
but touch the pages
with Desire and
grasp the Pen in Longing,
expecting He will Come.
He is both firm and
tender in asserting,

Come to Me,
Reach for Me.
Love Me.
Seek More of Me,
He beseeches.
Share Me.
Speak of Our alchemy.
Open your heart
to My Living Word,
My Reality, and
write of Me…

Write, Beloved.
Write.

ACKNOWLEDGEMENTS

Perhaps this is a book of self-forgiveness. Perhaps it is a manual for healing. It is a skinny broken finger which insists on pointing to Love, no matter how bent, or weak, or furious, *no matter what.* The love it points to is Jesus, or Jesse as I affectionately know Him. Jesse points right back.

I have been listening for love all my life. Childhood was a hypervigilant search for something true, for a sign that I am indeed, lovable. I have no doubt that feelings of unworthiness have precluded any evidence of awakening in these writings. I am no longer ashamed of that. I am grateful. Wounding and woundedness have been a paths of healing, ripening and teaching.

In this book, Jesse (Jesus) is the pivot point where I am connected to God, to humanity and to the Self that is Christ conscious and incarnate in the world. It represents years of holy instants where He has courted a fragile trust, invited endless questions, offered miracles and revelations, and always, always, sought More. He is both firm and tender in asserting His Desire for us.

I have not walked this path alone. There would be no book without Richard Dignan. Richard's friendship and support have been key to my offering the words herein. I have had intense doubt. He has had immeasurable belief, encouraging me to share both my process and the poetry. Insufferable ego attacks have been quelled as we read and reread these words together, with Richard seeing the value of the scribing before I could, helping me to accept the Source as true and valuable. Richard supported the book in every way, asking questions of Jess, planning retreats to share the words, and taking responsibility for the publishing. He is *all in.*

There are many others who knowingly or unknowingly helped bring these words to fruition, all of them part of the circle of my *Course in Miracles (ACIM)* family. Denise Fox and Katja Von Tiesenhausen gave generously, providing spiritual and financial support which helped me trust. They have given amazing faith to the value of these words. The cover art is the work of Nancy Schirmer, who is a beautiful work of Art in my life.

John Phillips, Cassandra Jean-Louis, Kathy Oremus and Pete Pedulla inspired and motivated me to put It out there. They have made sharing possible through technology and the nitty gritty volunteer work of establishing internet platforms.

Sincere thanks are owed to the Board of the Foundation of Open Hearts. This is our 501.c3 non-profit which offers retreats, events and sponsors our *ACIM* meetings each week. Penny Flanagan feeds our Foundation and gives tender care to our facilities. Alda Lyons has given hours to keeping our books. Don Baxter is a very present help at short notice, and has shared countless good words on behalf of these writings. They are indispensable. They are dear to me. There are others. The Board of the Foundation of Open Hearts has held me as I have been vulnerable in teaching.

Evelyn and John Ranfone, John Nagy, Bobby Vozzella, Julie Steller, Craig Oremus, Bernadette Eden, Fred Richards and many more are angels in the wings of this endeavor.

Finally, I want to thank Joe Pizziferri who personally heard Jesus tell him to *take care of me.* He has listened well. I love you Joey. I thank you. Jesse thanks you too.

marybeth

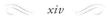

SECTION ONE
The Development of Trust

DIVE IN...

Go ahead.
Take the leap
    HERE!
Give yourself this sound byte.
It might save you.
It might pull you deep into
the arms of subconscious seas,
cloak you in the unbreathable quiet
of rooms beneath oceans.
It is willing to hold you
in perfect stillness;
all the waves of thinking
on the surface far above.

Don't be afraid.
Take one
    slow
        gentle
            breath.
And then
    submerge
        your
            heart.

There is Life
    below
        life.

There is Thought
    below
        thought,

a safe pocket of pure Being,
a no-place-calm-grace
that gives everything shamelessly.

Dive in.
Make a splash.
Move the surface with your decision.
Its little waves
will wash across the veneer-world
and touch somebody
while you rest in the Womb of God.

LITTLE MISSISSIPPI'S

(marybeth)
I sat in meditation this morning,
 surprised in the quiet
by an outburst from my eyes,
 and the deluge which came
like little Mississippi's,
 muddied by mascara,
overflowing from what source?
 Leaping from the smile lines
at the sides of my chin,
 they were sopped up in the pink
of my new waffle shirt.

I said His Name.
 Perhaps just the thought of Him
set the frost heaves to melting.
 It was Compassion
that came to meet me.
 Moments before I was wondering
about the direction my life could take;
 moments given to the burden
of responsibility and doubt.
 So many little thoughts come
and go in a breath.
 I scarce notice,
but then forsake them
 in an instant committed
purely to Jess.
 Or perhaps it is He
Who comes to rescue me

from these temptations.

My love is also pain, the flush of guilt
    the obvious imperfections
against His beauty;
    the lifelong longing
to fulfill His Plan,
    as if Jess were a man,
and my wanting to please Him,
    to accomplish a movement in hearts
which would validate His Life,
    which would raise the planet
if ever so slightly.
    Jesse's Plan has no steps.
I seek His sandals
    and do my best to grow these feet
to make them fit.
    I am like a mosquito taking on the wings
of an golden eagle.

I look upon my life, counting backwards
    the years of meditation,
of study and contemplation.
    I see none of that truly matters.
One moment in unthought supplication,
    one beat of unbridled dedication,
a Real acceptance not preceded by words,
    causes me to look through
the watery view and See
    the sun-crowned deck
beyond the double doors;
    the bare bones of lilac
dappled with clouds of snow;

the light glistening
through a common crystal
    splaying wreaths of color,
rings of rainbow from the window.

I understand,
    I have forgiven something,
and this world,
    a silent, shining, *Alleluia*.
I thank my tears
    for the little epiphanies
that remain
    after the rivers have run.
I thank Jesus.

Do Not Be Afraid

(Jess)

Do not take up your words, your swords,
to make anything happen
in the world you see.
Instead abide in Me.
Give time to Me.
Pause and rest in contemplation.
As every fearful picture rises
to tempt you,
turn again inside.
Be content to rest with My Words.

Do not try to figure out
why this or that is happening.
Do not try to prepare
for your betterment,
your plan, your journey.
There are many voices
seeking to be heard.
Listen only to My Voice.

You will know My Voice.
I am clear, certain, calm.
You will feel that
listening is resting,
listening is following,
flowing in My direction.
You will hold My Words
as a Presence
and they will fill you

with gratitude.
You will weep
because words of smallness,
anger and deprivation
will fall away.
Emotion's iron gates
will pull back
and reservoirs of untasted
feeling will wash through you,
disappearing.

Today you said to Me,
I am dying.
Do not be afraid.
This is a death of illusion,
of images and idols.
After this death
we know resurrection.

Remember this prayer:
The Father and I are One.
My will is the Will of the One
Who directs me.
There is no other Will,
There is only this Grace
expressed as my Life.

Remember God is full of surprises.
Because you have lived so long in darkness,
in the narrow tunnel of ego control,
surprise is frightening.
This is because ego fears God.
Remember the Spirit of the Son

is one of wonderment, enchantment.

Always stop to consider
what God is *really* up to…
She is always up to Her eyeballs
in eternal Love for you.

MIXED DESIRES:
THE TEPID TEA OF TEMPTATION

It is nearly impossible
    for you to reach for Me
with mixed desires,
    with a need to use
The Word
    to fix your life,
to fill your emptiness.
    These words are not given
to fill up your life
    but to empty the mind
of ego fixation.
    Mixed desires are
not true desires,
    not desires which
create.
    They cloud choice
with compromise,
    negating your
well-loved creations.
    Heart inspirations
are blanched by worldly
    recommendations
that undo originality,
    subverting brilliance,
diluting passionate potions
    of heart
with the tepid tea
    of temptation.
Would you please the world

or commit to Me?
I am not chiding
　　your attempts to serve
but ask you to consider
　　the power of
pure intention.

Consider the wish
　　for need fulfillment.
Consider what you believe
　　you **get** from Me.
Gladly I answer your call.
　　Enthusiastically I come
to guide you,
　　to warm your heart
with celestial Light.
　　Do look however,
at hidden objectives
　　for this scribing.
Purity of heart,
　　sincerity of soul,
the sweet, open
　　vulnerability of
unmitigated agendas
　　is the soil
where we deepen.

Your Words belong
　　to an unknown
divine Administrator,
　　the same Source that
pulls and draws breath

in and out,
filling and emptying
 the listening heart,
Whose only agenda
 is to serve Life,
giving and restoring
 where you would receive
My Voice and
 honor it as your own.
Let My Presence
 be welcomed
because you desire Me,
 because you Love Me.
Thoughts of *getting*
 subdivide your love
of Communication,
 calling for mercy.
We are *given* then
 to speak of forgiveness,
to remember Truth,
 and your wholeness
which can **get nothing**
 from the Love of God
because you ARE
 the Love of God.
What you are
 you have to give.
Offer this then,
 yourSelf to Me.
Offer your Love
 and name to Christ.
Offer the benediction

and fullness of life
eternally your own.

Come,
        because the Words
I offer
        draw you close,
bring you near
        to What we are
together.
        Transparent and clear
expression
        abides in the ear
of the heart we share.

I am moved
        by your longing
for Truth.
        It is indeed, cool,
calm water
        to the steaming city
of an overworked mind.
        Purify in Truth.
Sift your life
        for pretenses,
for obscured aims.
        See where desire
for Me parts
        from the drooling
deprivation of ego,
        who would grab
one more trophy

to glorify itself,
to prove its worth.
　　Less than valueless
is its poetry.
　　To use your phrase…
fluff.

Purify the heart
　　putting all your wishes
and God-given desires
　　in the hands of Holy Spirit,
your colander of true volition.
　　She washes everything
together,
　　your little propensities
toward self-elational wishing,
　　with the Will of Our Creator.
The false inclinations,
　　thin and weak
cannot last in her suds,
　　but slip away
leaving the real Call,
　　the deeper Love…
God coveted above all else.

My Word *is* Love.
　　You understand this
better than you
　　understand yourself.
My Presence is Real.
　　You feel this more
palpably than you have

felt false self.
Our communication here
    engenders your healing
and Our wholeness,
    which enables union
and fulfillment
    with all creation.
Shall we begin again
    with forgiveness for
the rambling,
the stumbling,
the tongue trodden into slavery
    by worldly ambition?
Here I am
    your peace,
    your perfection,
    your purity,
forever available
    to you who desire
the keys to the Kingdom;
    unattainable to
the mind split and broken
    in its capacity
to receive My revelation.
    Is not My Love
the revelation of God?
    Is not the revelation
of God
    the whole point of
our conversation?
    The quintessential
point of your life?

The superlative
Idea that joins us?
    And are you, *yourSelf*
not this very same Idea,
    the primogenial revelation
of your Creator,
    His unfolding mystery
of Being and Becoming?
    You are everything
Being,
    every promise fulfilled,
and everything *Becoming,*
    the incomprehensible
expanding, encompassing,
    infinite reach of Love.

Words are
    but pebbles
tossed from the dingy
    of your mind
onto the canvas of sea.
    Ripples billow out
in unceasing flow,
    almost imperceptibly.
Apart from God
    they lack substance,
creativity.
    But joined in Source
and Her Fervent Faculty,
    a little billow
becomes a Force,
    filling channels of
the open heart

with tidal Words
of Power.

Keep coming here
    knowing you are
dear to Me,
    combing the confusion
with nets of faith,
    for the crown of Light
and the gentle Breath,
    Who seeks your lungs,
Who wills our Oneness.
    Spirit comes upon you
and is with you,
    and is You.
These Words you create,
    now create your Life.

Keep Me close
    and be willing always
to make every influence,
    every stride, every need
an altar
    where I can kneel with you
in forgiveness.
    In this way
we glorify Our Father.
    He waits upon your clarity
sending a perpetual Call,
    strident in His Desire
and unconditional Love
    for You,
Who ever shall Be

His heart-felt Creation,
His *Self,* His Soul.
Place your mouth,
your voice,
into Source Superintendence,
and let the Son
shine forth
His simple, holy Truth.

SOFTEN THE BRITTLE BITTERNESS

(Jess)
Whenever you're ready
    I AM.

Is it alright if I am a little playful?
It has been a very serious weekend for you.
I am grateful for your intense focus.
I am grateful that you are *all in*.
And yet I invite you to consider this:
Intensity is of the ego.
There is no tension in Me.
Christ is peace.
Peace is not passive, but neither is it tense.
And I have been known to tell a good joke now and then.

My heart is Light.
Be you happy too.
The closer you come to Home
the less intense it gets.
Tension is friction. Joining is fluid.
Peace is consummation, melting boundaries,
surpassing the rigid with a new chemistry.

Alright we begin now softer, easier,
without any goal apart from our communion.
The fusion of souls is not a collision
but a chemistry which ignites the heart.

I have touched you there (the heart) just now.
I have brushed my fingers against the door.
I have brought the fire. I am fanning the flames.

Allow My warmth. Truly I am here.
I will not fail you.
Clarify, sift through the clouds.
Enter the chamber.
Share My breath.
We are at home together in the nest.

You want to talk about your weekend.

(marybeth)
Yes

(Jess)
But then I see you want to avoid some deep truth,
some things you prefer not to address;
some things are still quite difficult to face.
How easy it would be to turn away these deeper lessons.

(marybeth)
I don't want to know about all the wrong in me.

(Jess)
Thoughts arise like graffiti from a moving train.
You decide what you see,
what to believe,
which you will claim.
You determine to invest your faith,
or pull the chain that stops the racing engine.

Today you put Your holiness,
your divine love on display,
made it a target of a top dog interrogation.
Who would play with Reality this way?

Who would be critic to Heaven?

I do not judge as you judge.
I do not measure how well I have done,
or you have done.
Perfection does not have a Spiritual IQ.
(Neither do you.)
Perfection is simple.
We do not *think back*
was God *good* today? was God *bad?*

God is Perfection small mind cannot comprehend.
On earth, perfection is our meaning and our purpose,
the purpose of the self to realize its God-Being
through heart, thought, and body.
Perfecting like this is unrelated to your judgments
of good or bad. It is Reality.
Our perfect self is communication and creation.
Our perfect self is beyond evaluation.
Our perfect self is Love's expression,
an extension that cannot be contained in form,
yet formed all life of Its illumined Mind.

What you are, understands these words
and by your embrace,
they become the perfect,
living grace of God birthing
through your writings.

But see how you project
abominable judgments on your holiness.
If you are capable of judging your holiness,
you are judging their holiness.

I tell you, you are judging Me.
I have guided you to behold them, not see them.
I have invited you to cultivate a spirit of wonder,
not allegation. And I am guiding you now
to accept the flame, the fire, the power of Love.
Relax the critical battleax
that doggedly hacks these scribings.

You need not pick yourself apart.
You need not decide success from failure.
You need not determine how to move ahead.
The perpetual fire of forgiveness
burns the dross of mortal thinking.
The fire is My passion, and My pathway to your heart.
It is soft, gentle, but exceedingly focused.
My fire burns as desire for Truth.
Truth is a judge of justice.

Your willingness to be an *unknower,*
an undecider, undoes the never done
that you have mistaken as reality
and accepted as personal evidence
of your being born wrong!

How I miss you when you douse My flames
in the icy heart of unforgiveness.
How you miss Me keeping yourself in the cold,
locked out of the Love Which abides within.

Our Father has given us His Light, His inner Son,
His radiant exuberance of Life.
I offer this Son to you.
It is greater than the orb of your daylight star.

It is the Source of all life, all fire.
Its Truth is all enveloping holiness.
Take this gift from me tonight.
Let the Son of the Heart of the Cosmic Conflagration
burn small thinking on the pyres of forgiveness.
Let the torch of My Wisdom set fire to your blood
igniting streams of awe-full passion.

Your vocation, my beloved friend, is cherished.
Feel My Love for you and continue to follow.
Love's Purpose is Light, is Fire,
is Joy, always only Joy.
Love bears no resemblance to your noisy protests
about the nature of these writings.
Love bears no scale to weigh your failures.
Love is creation.
It has not eyes for graffiti that defiles.

Listen and soften the bitter brittleness
against your worthiness.
Your own thoughts are purposeless.
Now, write beloved.
Write.

I Do Not Know What Forgiveness Means

In the flare of a pain body, I contemplated the *23rd Psalm*. It is part of my meditation ritual. The words, *you anoint my head (and my heart) with oil, were experienced* as the palpable touch of Jesse's Hand upon me, and that anointing in turn extended to the person who was the object of my anger.

(marybeth)
I am sorry
for what I have believed
and done
in light of those beliefs.

I am sorry,
my heart bowed in wonder
that love could be stolen,
contorted and distorted
into needs and demands.

I am sorry
for the loss of truth,
the wavering,
the scarcity that engendered
manipulation;
that plans for my happiness
were prescribed by the ignorance
of egotistical-mind.

I am sorry,
unhappy about my
woundedness,

a victim of
my own volition.
Sorry for the pains
and persecution
I have mindlessly
inflicted.

I am sorry
for all I have done
in the name of
self-satisfaction
and in reaction
to fear.
I am sorry
for what I yet
fear to do,
fear to give,
fear to show up
to live as real *Self.*

I am sorry mostly
that the hours,
the words,
the Great Love
has been made to wait,
has been cast aside
and what I have
projected upon it
cost me precious life
without the vital Voice
of His perfect Will,
His intimate Guidance.

I do not know what
forgiveness means.

(Jess)
This morning
you accepted
the anointing.
Through the Psalm
you received the oil,
the cross upon
your brow, your heart.
As I blessed you,
you thought to extend
that blessing,
anointing the one
you most wanted
to hate.

I was there
as you reached
for his third eye,
gently signing
the symbol of the Trinity;
as you reached deeper –
beyond
and touched his heart,
where I touched your heart
with the sign
of the Holy Threesome.
Father, Son, Spirit,
you called Them,
feeling great love

and longing
that your enemy
would experience
freedom from the salt
of your anger
and ill will.
You thought to
offer him peace.

This anointing,
this simple willingness
to bring God into
relationship
is forgiveness.
To welcome Me in
is to change the goal
from sin
to holy winsomeness.

Remember I came close
and you felt My kiss
upon your brow,
and you accepted
My lips;
your body
shuddered slightly
with palpable effects,
breathing in My Presence,
allowing the Touch
to once again
expose your mercy.

You gave yourself
to Me
as you gave him
your soul blessing,
and then you wept,
crying for all the
hurt remembered
and for the freedom
so gently, sweetly
accepted and received.

Here is forgiveness
from your willingness –
from your powerful desire
that Love touch everyone,
even those upon whom
you have projected
your smallness,
your anger.

Love prevails
in your *wanting* to love.
Your willful remembering
calls Us in
to fulfill that desire
because We know
the purity of all souls.
We hold the key to
innocent-mindfulness.

We are happy
to join at your altar
to inspire the

alchemy of humanity
with Truth,
to witness
the ascendancy of souls
in a holy instant
where you ask
to see him differently,
and place the kiss of Love
upon the heart
you would have healed,
literally sealed
with a kiss, the wounds
of ancient enmity.

Forgiveness is
this moment's potency
for holy awakening,
the purity of your intention
lifted high,
at-one-ment alive;
you become the Eucharist
infused with Light –
and the fullness of
the Holy Family sings
a song of addition,
a song of completion.

Listen deep,
listen far back
into the Womb
of Creator.
Praise farther forward

into the More of His realms.
Hear the simple Psalm
you offered this morning
at the altar of charity
unfolding into poetry,
the sound of beginner Mind,
the Thought of which shines
with clemency,
selflessness,
faith and
humility.

This morning
We are grateful
for the witness
of forgiveness,
the blessedness
of the reason for
Our gathering
together,
and the meeting of
a brotherhood in Love
at your altar.

MERELY A SERVANT?

I was feeling my weakness, the temptations that flirt with flesh and the needs that cause me to feel lack. I was seeing how these feelings, if not exposed, could compromise my choices and behaviors. I offered them to Christ in search of strength, but in the offering I felt resistance. The idea arose that my only capability was servitude. It was uncomfortable, the idea of God as Master and marybeth as servant. It felt uncreative, small, and stifling. I asked Jess, *Am I merely the servant of a supreme Master? Is that the spiritual life?*

(Jess)
You, the mind, body and hands serve,
not in enslavement but like an instrument
perfected to carry the incorporeal
unutterable beauty of Heaven's notes.
You are perfected, directed and disciplined
to hold what cannot be held
without the passion, intent and will
to allow celestial chords
to reverberate your humanity.
The Master redesigns and sculpts you,
polishes you, shaping you into the flute,
canvas, word or sculpture that brings forth,
exudes, presents and pronounces
the utmost expression of Reality.

Now…
You, the Soul, are also One with Me,
I, Who holds the chisel, Who is the sound.
Infused with Source, I, the impersonal
pours through, divinizing, sacratizing,
potentizing, poeticizing and illuminizing

human experience into Christed life,
God become personal on earth.

Yours is a stellar gift, the greatest part,
being both an experience of instrument and Sound.
As you let Me Master, we share the glory and joy
of Heaven's refrain on earth. But see,
you are as much Master as you are server,
as much Creator as you are created,
as much Wisdom as the word,
as much the Name of God as the pronunciation,
as much the Breath as the flute.
Is that merely a servant?
Take a deep breath.

I Can Be Trusted

On the May flower Full Moon

(Jess)
Soften the brow.
Soften the heart.
Soften the breath.
I go before you.
I can be trusted.

I have been in the midst
of trouble before
and untroubled
have given you reason
to unfurl the ridges
that line your face.

I know what to do.
I restore, I embrace
the helpless.
I hear you.
I can be trusted.

How does the Lover
come close
when you are hard,
rigid,
unyielding to His touch?
Look at the defense
that costs you so much,
that costs you the love
that impassions your life,

that leaves you defunct
a fatigued and fruitless vine.

Soften the mind.
Soften the eyes.
Butter the bread
of communion
with your life

wide open,
with your consent,
with a **yes.**
Give me all the rest.

Give me the discontent,
the fear, the doubt,
the beatings on your breast,
of frustration.
Lean upon My Strength.
I will gird you up.
I will draw you in.
I am open,
a hidden tunnel
giving way
as you tumble
into welcome,
into Word,
unlike the judge
who abuses
the tenderness
you offer,
who shreds the gifts
you give into raw

and ragged threads.
I am gently exalted
in your precious-
depthless softness.

Soften the brow.
Soften the heart.
Soften the breath
and let Me love you.
Let Me Love you *strongly*.

Resist not My Love.
But love Me without defense.
I assure you I have a Plan.
Have I said it plainly enough?
I can be trusted.

SECTION TWO

Vulnerability in
Relationship with Jesse

CONSIDER THE POSSIBILITIES

...if individuals will not consider in their consciousness the possibilities of that which God's life will do unto them, how can they receive the out breathing of His ineffable Love? Serapis Bey

Consider the possibility of that which God's Life will do unto you.
You must consider this in the depths of your heart
in order to receive His Breath (Ruah) as your own...
in order to *ascend* in consciousness toward the God-Design
Which is the Divine within your humanity.

Do not be fooled by the word ascend.
We are not literally going up.
We are going within to a vibration of higher purity.
We are lifting up our consciousness into His Joy,
His Lightness of Being,
where every possibility is absent of fear.

Consider the possibility of all that will be done
through you as you rise into His Holy Power,
(the power of Atonement).

The God-Life is your Real Life
Whose Being within necessitates
purity and universal awareness of Itself
in all living things.
The wonder of all the possibilities of
this Purity-Awareness is the infinite
power of Creator sons.

FORGETFULNESS AND THE
PATH OF RELATIONSHIP

(Jess)
What beats your heart?
What gives you life?
We forget what is closer
than the iris to the eye.

It is a naked birth
and a naked death.
Not even our bodies
are in our keeping.
Our vulnerability
is so great!

Humanly defenseless,
we are powerless to control
the destiny, the effects
of a world apart from Source.
But clothed in Spirit,
abiding in Presence,
the iris gives the eye
Its Sight.
Sight gives might to change,
from outer-space
to inner grace
from darkest night to light.
Are you willing to dwell in Light?

You who seek His Way,
His Breath,
Who feel His Love

within your breast,
you have chosen to See.
Your part is more intense,
more difficult than
the ascetic, the monastic,
whose rituals and denials
become sleepy canisters
for peace,
though peace in part.
You who choose realization
in a world of noise,
of mayhem,
of blaring discombobulation,
have chosen the path
of relationship.
Though addiction, and delay
and heart break pave your way,
You are given to transcend,
given to transform,
Bearers of heaven's plan on earth...
listen raptly now.

I give you inspiration
to forgive, to remember.
I give you the power of
the holy relationship.

Through filiation
we restore the Christ on earth,
healing the arrogance
of individual specialness,
the mistake of self-creation,

the pains of a rabid
and wrong identification.

I have said, *Be happy,*
for I have overcome the world.
It was complete union
with the indwelling Spirit
that raised Me above
the marsh of human senility.
It is the same Spirit,
the Comforter,
I gave to the disciples,
given you now,
a Spirit of Love
that you **will** to remember,
realize and extend,
as It **Wills** to remember You,
as you have been forgiven
as you **will** to change
your point of view.
As you remember them
you remember Me
and I the key to the *Self*
you forgot.

It exhausts you
this determination
to overcome a world alone.
Alone is a request for weariness.
Yet I keep my promise.
Together we overcome
the pains and perjuries

of the very relationships
that seem to blot
your joy and freedom,
and cover your innocence
like sprawling mold.

As you desire to *behold* them,
so it is you know Me,
and the long sought state
of supernal intimacy.
Have you not cried out
for intimacy,
suffering the blisters
on heart's tongue
from the desert
of what relationship
has become in separation?

The consent to Union
is relief for this thirst,
the primordial vulnerability
in which you See your mistakes,
your resistance,
your pure and perfect Existence.

So doing, the world is overcome.
Your life rooted in Christ
reaches to bless,
to embrace, to become
the Kingdom of Love on earth,
one by one by one,
with every son I send you.

And every son returned to Me,
to be re-Seen,
unveils indwelling God,
consistently re-created
through Our remembrance and revelation,
forever vital if you choose the portal
of relationship reborn in Christ.

What then is forgetfulness?
You stand on a cliff
teeter-tottering in the dark,
though Light would pour forth
from every portal of your heart,
shutters barred with forgetfulness.
You choose not to See
where you stand, and feign
a façade of balance,
thoroughly exhausted.

You stand in a crowd,
inner noise surround sound,
fear and worry the companions
with whom you converse.
Are you not lost
to Peace, to Poise,
though I rest in your heart,
waiting for your call?
Waiting for the doors of defense
to fly apart?
Waiting for recognition,
the admission of your addiction
to judge as it exiles the soul.

You sail upon a sea
of small and fleeting pleasures,
discovering small mind
is a dinghy without oars.
An ocean swells and roars
and the good you sought to find
obscured,
the Love you sought to find,
unfound.
How much time
will you give
to these waters?
How much trust
to a world
devoid of Christ?

Forgetfulness is not a sin,
but a path of blindness,
a weakness of heart,
a spot of ink
on a spotless white cloth.
Have I not stated,
the Kingdom is within?
And does your inner abode,
your perfect heart
not have a King of 20/20 Vision?
Ah… as you would say,
a Queen. A Sophia,
Who must like this be canvassed
before the hour of crisis,
before the darkness falls…

Be my Guide,
Be my Vision,
Be my Answer,
Be my Queen,
Be my Power,
Be my Presence,
Be my Only, Everything.

Into your Relationship,
Into this holy encounter
She comes.
She rules with Heart.
She reigns as Love.
She Looks and Sees
with holy awareness
You Who are **not** sleeping;
and night has recoiled because
you joined your Mind,
you recalled your Will.
Darkness has abated
because you chose to remember,
letting Her Power Be.
I have whispered, you have listened.
The sounds you hear,
full faithfulness,
The soul that sighed
rises unto Me,
and questions fade into Day.

Washing Feet

A Holy Thursday

(marybeth)
Slipping off my sandals, I peel away a bit of skin.

A bit of death
between the toes
insists on sticking.
I reach to grab it
noticing then
the thickness
of my nails,
the shadows of gray,
evidence of fungal life.
I shudder at the thought
of a parasite
growing in the folds
of my feet.
And more,
the shame,
the wonder and blame
of feet unsightly
in his gaze.

The neglect and busyness
of my life
is reflected here,
a reason for rejection
and fear
apparent here,
on this big toe

bent with time.
I wonder how to hide
the damages,
the ugliness.
It is too late.
He is before me
and within me,
around and
through me,
sensing my shame,
bowing low,
knees to stone,
taking my feet in his hands,
Oh God, caressing my sole!

Heat rises in my checks.
He is pouring the water,
a flow of soft light.
The God in his hands,
stroking, holding tight.
I want to hide
from this ablution
but this water
cleans inside,
and every defense
submitted,
every pride given
to the peace
and the purpose
of the night.

A badgering thought,

I am not worthy.
I want to reverse
everything,
bathe His feet,
caress His toes,
kneel low in the Presence
and glow of generosity.

Without a word,
he makes me understand
this demonstration is a gift,
a lesson in servantship,
leadership that bows Its head
and genuflects
recognizing the ones
that belong to us.
I belong to Him
and feel the conversion,
my unworthiness becoming
a steward to His Greatness,
my reluctance becoming
the Will of God
that sons of men
may turn within
and find a fountain there.

I feel His Love.
I feel anointed,
apostled and appointed
to forgive the foul.
But who am I to believe
that I could set men free?

Finally he rises,
the tallest of angels (!)
with a
a bowl,
a towel
and a kiss.
Prompting me to minister,
wide eyes reveal His bliss.
I hear Him say,
Lead this way,
This is a path of strength.

I Am Vulnerable

(marybeth)
I share personal, spiritual, experiences.
I share life lessons,
the whacks and the miracles.
I share deeply from my heart.
Sharing brings all kinds of reactions.
Most people think relationship
with God should be private.
Most people fear talking about
the wounds they've discovered,
the ego traps they are suffering.
Most people are afraid. They think
what they think is wrong or worse, crazy.
I think this too. I fear I will be judged.
Maybe that's because we all judge
each other. Judgment *is* crazy making.

Are you afraid to look at and think
deeply about your life, your soul,
your feelings, mistakes and desires?
Are you afraid to be quiet?
Quiet brings anxiety. Quiet brings
to light what needs our attention.
It has taken me a lifetime to
really look for God, to *really* look at Her.
Most of us accept a semi-palatable
version of Deity offered by institutions
or tradition, or self-help books.
She is not a Being of intimacy.

We are shallow.
We live in shallow mind.
We like staying at the surface of life.
We live wanting someone else to learn for us.
We live in fear of other dimensions.
We live in fear of a Creator.
We live in darkness, isolation,
afraid to discover what is just under
the armor of the heart.
We are afraid of Love.
Being afraid of Love is being afraid of God.
Who can understand what we
are afraid to look at?

Once Jess said to me,

My heart longs
    to behold
in your eyes
    the reflection of
My Passion.
    Yet must you look!
You must lift up your gaze
    and bring your eyes
to meet Me,
    as I have come again…

Imagine if in my shame I looked away.
Imagine if in my fear I closed my eyes.
Imagine if all I could do was look
at my feet and tremble when He said,
    Look directly at Me.
I would have missed Love!

I would have missed God!
So now, I look and I share
and take time to *feel* deeply.

I share experiences that are
abnormal to most.
I share thoughts
that are almost incomprehensible
except that those willing to KNOW
recognize Truth in what I say.
Sometimes people will talk about
my writings and say,
Boy she has a lot of issues.
Sometimes they want to fix me.
Sometimes they extend pity.
And then there are those
who do not want me to embrace
my wounds and my humanity.
They want me all the time to say,
I am the Christ.
And I do say that.
I say, *I am the Christ, marybeth,*
one with Christ, Jesus.
His love of humanity took him to the cross,
a journey not unlike our own,
where the blows of a thousand lifetimes
are being brought to light and healed,
where the wounds of multi-millions
are projecting their archetypical illusions
as a world of make believe.
It is for my personal healing,
correction and Atonement.

It is so we waken to the Christ in us.
And we are all healing together.

I am vulnerable.
Vulnerability is not shameful.
These flaws and faults
and foibles I find inside me,
are inside you too. Only I am looking
with wonder at what I made. I am
looking with compassion at how hard
it is to be human *and* divine. I am
daring to dig for the ugly, broken part
of my mind, deceptively hidden
in the folds of psyche, making all our lives
robotic, hypnotic, reactionary.
Our small minds are virtually
preprogramed, predestined software,
without a single original idea!
In that package is birth and death.
That is not an Original Idea.
That is another mindless limit.
I am looking to be free from all
the kool aid life has offered me.
I have accepted a lot of crap
and made it flesh.
I am looking to heal
what is not true
because healing reveals God.

I am looking for God, actively, openly.
I don't care if people think I am mental.
It doesn't matter. God matters.

Waking up matters.
Revelation matters.
You matter too.
So....

What are you doing with the mess
of *your* life?

A Course in Miracles says, the ego is so
ingeniously invasive to the whole of our thinking
that we do not **even begin** to see it.
Its enveloping reach extends from silent scripts,
trauma, and past learning within.
It is a like mental fly paper,
attracting all that buzzes
holding it hostage. But…
It never gets to the source of all those bugs.
We give it our faith because,
somewhere along the line,
it seemed to help with our pain,
or frustration, or worry.
It seemed to control the chaos.
It offered us a nice cold beer
to solve our problem of insecurity
but then added the problem of addiction.

Ego mind taught us **to look away**
from the angst inside,
We are not to feel our pain.
We are definitely not to communicate
our deepest, most authentic feelings.
We listened and gave it authority.
We let it run our lives.

We flipped a switch and said,
you decide for me.
From then on we were trapped.
We couldn't even see the choice
we had made to abdicate power
to a covert thought system that is not us,
but feigned persona as our life.

What I've found in my sub-humanian journey is,
at some dissociated level, we don't want to
BE WHO WE ARE IN TRUTH!
But that sounds insane, and it is
because all we really want is the freedom
to be the love we are in Truth.
Better said,
we have grown comfortable being masked.
We have grown used to it.
We have grown away from Reality.
We are snoring loudly.
Vulnerability exposes that.
Sharing with others helps me recognize
I am in a sinking submarine of fallacious belief.
Sharing raises me up, delivers me to Truth.
I love exploring God.
But I can't if ego is in charge of my expedition.
Ego doesn't know God.
Ego, the comprehensive thought system
of fear and doubt that masquerades
as me, doesn't KNOW anything.
It is a false self, living a false life,
using a false name.
Does anyone want to see that?

Does anyone want to admit that?
I do. I must. Freedom depends on it.

This week I sat on my trusty couch
and took a good look at the nature of sickness.
I have had a bruiser of a head cold.
Sick of being sick, I wanted to understand
the source, the cause of this attack on the body.
My Friend was eager to respond to the call.
Together we went within, deeper perhaps
than I have gone before.
He says it is almost impossible for us
to really look at the extensive rule of ego.
It is truly difficult to see
our immoral, sullied, selfish,
twisted, duplicitous thoughts.
We don't believe we have such tendencies.
Most of us are blind, closed,
living an ignorance that is **never** bliss.

But I caught a glimpse.
Really it was just a little peek,
as if folds of darkness were being peeled back.
I caught a pocket of wants, demands, needs,
that is a certain selfishness,
ugly, privileged, bourgeois.
I also saw the image of myself striving,
pushing to be somebody. It was a false self,
a pretend person ruled by appetites and wanna-be-ism.
It needed a pretty cover to feed its demands.
The appearance is a posture of manipulation
and a thought of getting. It is lack.

It is the opposite of beauty.
It is fake, illusion, and yet,
I saw it operating and controlling my life.
Many choices, many plans have been
made blindly by this thought system.
Indeed, it was so deep, I could barely
keep my focus. It is slippery.
Right now, I am working hard
to give adequate expression
to its insidious nature.

Afterward I felt it was grace that
gave me understanding. It was illumination.
I know I cannot simply "forgive it."
I know I do not have
the capacity to change it.
I only realize that Awareness is
uncovering darkness.
Awareness is the light
that shines away all lies.
Awareness is a waking state.
Awareness is the Eye of God.
As Jess says, *the Eye that looks*
and sees nothing at all.
How odd that I believe,
nothing has usurped my freedom.

I am vulnerable, open, alive,
and approaching freedom through these words,
through the will that seeks Truth,
through the heart that wants God above all else
and would heal every obstacle to fulfillment.

Let me truly desire freedom.
Let me be an ally of Awareness.
Let me truly want Truth.
Let me look for God everywhere,
even if it means exposing parts of me
I'd rather forget. I'd rather reject.
Let me find **Reality** by communicating
as authentically as possible with you,
whom I believe is wise in vulnerability too.

LET IT FLOW DOWN

(Jess)
Let it flow down.
Let it be joy.
You are worthy.
Allow every chakra
to pop with delight,
with freedom from
constriction
that The Word of God may flow
through –
that this Word
may be felt-experience,
the palpable present practice
of My Substance
pouring into manifestation
into your life,
into your very body,
into the cells,
into the hairs on your head.
Are you willing
to EXPERIENCE this Word,
this vibrancy,
this Light infused with the temple
so that your Life Itself
flows as My Body?
How much do I want
this communion with you!

I am here.
Do not fear Me.

This is not some alien
mystical takeover.
This is the Love of Your Life
seeking true communion
with the child – Greater Rays
now available to you
and through you shared.
This living-breathing Poem of God
perfumes the garden of earth.
All creation inhales
Its in-sense,
awakening hearts of stone,
melting old bones of resentment.
Can you not Vision
the transformation?
How beautiful everyone
and everything will look to you?
Like pillars of rock
once again become
children of a Grandpoppi
of incomprehensible Love.

(marybeth giggles)

(Jess)
Is this too much for you?

(marybeth)
It's a bit way out.

(Jess)
We will move together
at your pace

but soon the feeling
of My Love will so
inhabit your life
you will sorely miss
moments apart from
The Word.
I am grateful
that you accepted
the plan this morning. (Richard's)
Trust Me.
Trust Me more than
these pithy thoughts
that you have called trust.
My promise is Real.
It is this you will teach.
My promises are eternal.
Is it this I Will you to Live.
My promises are good.
(Pause, Breathe, Reflect)

Consider this then
the turning of the first page
and again I say,
Let it flow joy.
Our communion,
our union,
is My greatest joy,
and as we are
drawn evermore deeply
into The Word – Alive,
it shall be so for
you and for those

who hear
and Love The Word of God.

I give you My Word on this.
My Word is My Promise.

Die a Little While with Me

(Jess)
Die to self now.
Die a little while
with Me.

> Come deeper.
> Allow each little lock
> of each iron shackle
> to be popped.

Come freely to Me,
freely to the Word
Which joins us.

> Come without expectation
> or fear,
> only appear here
> where Wisdom holds a place
> for you,
> where the heart breathes
> one gently effervescent
> light of Peace.

Grant Me access
to your Kingdom
by letting go of all
that binds you
to doubt, to fear.
I cannot enter there.

> I am here now,

Beloved of you,
beloved of God.
Ask of Me What You Will.
This is not a question
for a genie in a bottle,
for what you Will
is one with God,
and I can only give
What You Will truly-
the Will within You
shining as it has
from Beginning Mind.

You need not ask
again and yet again
to fulfill the Plan,
to take your place
among the ministers of God.
Your place is established.
Your worthiness
already given.
You came in
to serve this Plan
already anointed,
already holy,
and only your awareness lacking,
only the doubts of the world
impinging upon
the smooth functioning
of your true purpose.

Peel those veils
from the heart

and understand,
the eternal vow
remains unbroken–
God unmoved by
anything you might
say or do
in alliance with
the co-opter/the tempter.
Tear these veils
of illusion about
having left Me – or
even the possibility
of leaving Me.

I am here.
I am forever.
We are the Son of God,
the Light that cannot be put out,
the Eye that never closes
unto darkness,
the holy creation,
the same yesterday,
today and tomorrow.

Speak earnestly with Me
now.
Speak with your heart
naked.
Speak to Me from the voice of
Desire.
Speak of your vows
and your fears of keeping these vows,
of your daylight and your darkness.

Each word will I take
as prayer,
each word as your promise
and faithfulness,
each word like a
tiny caterpillar
whose spinning
into the cocoon
of My perfect safety
shall bloom,
the metamorphosis
of your humanity
into the beauty,
the fullness of flight
that follows the burgeoning wings
of the butterfly.

> Certainly I am here
> to bring certainty to your part.
> Write of Me from your heart.
> Trust that.

DARE TO ASK FOR A MIRACLE
The Law of Wonder

This piece was written as I sat with Richard prior
to a retreat. I am sick with a head cold.

(Jess)
I am healing you
>as your healing
heals Me.
>How can that be?
Your healing
>does not occur
in separation.
>Healing, even of the body,
occurs in joining.
>As you join with Me
this morning,
>you are willing unity.

Unity is a whole-hearted
>state of Being.
Your whole heart is given
>unto the holy Heart
of Our communion.
>My Whole Heart
receives you,
>joins your will,
the space between us closing,
>the little gap
where sickness feigned power
>to keep us apart
now empty.

So that reaching out for Me
　　your heart expands.
　　The doors shut tight
with *I can't*
　　fly open,
your capacity to receive My Word
　　enhanced.
Health, happiness, holiness
　　are welcomed in.

Do you dare
　　ask for a miracle?
Would your risk
　　disappointment,
even despair
　　in the fear
of unfulfilment?
　　Come close now.
Let me show you how to approach
　　Our Father.
He wills you suffer not,
　　not a hair on your head,
nor the stub of a toe...
　　His Own Health
the only design
　　for His beloved.
Call upon His Will
　　and ask of His Desire.
Call upon His Love
　　and seek Its Beneficence.
In this moment
　　where you perceive time
an obstacle,

and bodies seem to run
another course,
    let mind rest in My correction.
Dare to ask
    for a miracle.

To ask of Me
    is to abide
in the Law of Wonder.
    The Law of Wonder
leads the curious heart
    to states of Mind
as yet unknown to you.
    To ask for a miracle
is **not** to determine
    what you need,
    what grace should give,
    when it should happen.
But ask by putting
    all your questions
into My open Hands.
    Inquire of My
everlasting Love
    to reach to You,
to raise you into
    your *Real Self,*
the Answer to every
    conceivable problem.

To ask for a miracle
    is to refrain from asking
all other questions
    but one.

What is Your Will for me Father(?)
    putting aside every worry,
every care,
    turning your heart
into an open field
    of possibility,
quieting your mind,
    seeking the release that is assured
as you turn to Me.

Dare to ask for a miracle.
    Allow all of the fearful sensations
to arise and pass.
    Watch with devotion
for Love's appearance.
    Appeal no more.
Trust and linger
    in quiet gratitude.
It knows
    Your Father loves you.
And I, blessed Friend,
    Love to Love you too.
My joy is to inspire you
    to unimaginable heights
of trust,
    openheartedness,
to increase your belief in
    Our limitless potential
and decrease your allegiance
    to sickness and worry.

Consider this
    as you clutch that ailment

like a long lost buddy,
    would you lose this companion
and dare to be your Self?

    Would you dare to **Be**
the miracle
    of your life long quest?
Indeed, in Truth you are,
    the maximally expressed
Love of Our Father.

SECTION THREE
Deeper

Stop Wiggling, Rest

(marybeth)
How many times today have you felt frustration?
How many times did you rush, hurry,
your eyes focused on the future,
your heart blind to the witnesses of love
right where you are?
> **Where you are** is Answer.
> **Where you are** is Holy.
But who can hear God speak
when ears are tuned to Channel Negativity?
> W O R Y.
That's an ***am*** station with an ego DJ.

Soul yearns for peace. Ego screams, not now.
Ego wants anything and everything ***but*** now.
Now would hurl ego into oblivion.
Now is what you truly want.
Now is where Your Love is... always has been.

Our *Course* lesson today gives us words
to help us ***own*** what we truly want.
We want Love. Fear wants us.
We want Truth. The Liar wants us.
What will you choose? Fear or Love?
What do you really want?

Repeat after me,
I will not be afraid of Love today. *ACIM WBP2- 282*
This is a choice, a decision to recognize What I am,
and all that longs to belong to me.
I am a holy child of God.

Love is mine.

Maybe I can rest HERE a moment and accept it.

A few weeks ago I was running helter skelter
futzing in a million directions.
The whole time I was yelling at Jess,
demanding He give me peace.
Suddenly I heard Him yell back!
That was so unlike the soft spoken shepherd
of my meditations. It shocked me into awareness.

(Jess)
I am offering you the way of peace,
but I cannot give it to you
unless you pause to receive it.
Stop telling me all about your frustration.
Stop running around asking for My help.
Sit down and listen.
Let Me Be in charge.
I assure you I can handle the responsibility.
Give Me your trust.
Stop wiggling.
Rest.

I will not be afraid of Love today,
neither fear Truth or Peace,
nor the Voice for God,
but rest.
Rest… that too He will give to me.

LET ME REMEMBER YOU

(marybeth asks Jess for a message on her birthday. She asks to remember God.)

(Jess)
Would silence be alright?
Would you trust Me deeper
moving past words
into the sublime plume
of quiet?

All words, all voices
disappear,
as you listen…
as every ear
in every cell
of your being
opens to hear
the imperceptible,
between breaths,
with you
plunging into
nothingness,
into spaces
where nothing
offers something;
traveling in
soft search
which falls away
to peace,
and *still* I invite you
deeper,

into felt experience
of stillness,
a stillness alive,
an ever so gently
quivering anticipation
and delegation to
What is there
in the deep.

You think perhaps
you have not succeeded
in unearthing
a proper message,
a message worthy
of a long-time devotee?
What do I know of years?
I call you to touch
the face of eternity.
I present the One
Who folds time
together,
revealing what is behind
the minutes and instants
you give in prayer –

FEEL.

Let your heart feel
through the dark.
Behind the eclipse
there is
Brilliance
Beyond

Belief,
the unspoken
eternal Message
of your Creation,
the remembrance
of the Womb
of Word.

Do not try too hard.
Unengage your mind.
Remembering is merely
settling into
the Universal Frequency,
tuning the heart
to the Desire for Truth
and finding yourself
aware of *YourSelf.*

SOMETHING FROM NOTHING

(Jess)
You remember your grandmother,
her love of the kitchen,
how she had this gift,
taking a little aiolo, olio, and oregano,
(Italian foods I do not know how to spell),
seemingly making something
out of nothing.

You relished
those moments.
How easy it was for her
to create a delicious meal,
her deep smile
of pleasure
even wider
as you loved it.
The tastes and sensations
were so rich!
You had a wish
to be like her,
to make something wonderful
of what you felt to be
meagre resources,
to touch people
to their core
with delicacies of love.
Yours as yet
unmade, untasted,
you wondered

from where will they come?

Would you agree
nothing
was the ingredient
that gave your grandma's meals
the abundant praise
and appreciation they deserved?
Nothing
in the cupboard,
nothing
in the refrigerator.
Empty
as far as you could tell
but for a bowl of oil,
and a grating of Locatelli;
nothing
to *really* cook with,
an uninviting void.
Yet you had to admit
out of nothingness
came something,
not just anything,
but something
uniquely creative
and nourishing,
something
that brought
you together
at the table
mmmming
like drunken gurus.

This was magic.
This was art,
not merely cooking,
not nearly a craft
but ingenious,
original, resourceful,
a remedy
for our hunger,
and our impoverished beliefs.

I tell you now
this Creativity
resides in you,
the magical capacity
to bring forth
from your love
a treasure,
satisfying and replete,
a Thought of plenty;
a feast
that does not stop
at your table,
but is loaves,
daily bread
for countless
hungry children,
fishes for the famished.

Your something
fills bellies
and hearts rejoice
at repast,

savoring the meal,
coming back for seconds
though it stays with you
forever.

Something
from the seeming nothingness
of silence,
Something
from the perceived emptiness
of quiet,
Something
from these moments
as you retire
to Our kitchen
to seek Love's recipe;

indwelling,
a seeming absence
of resource.
Yet will you
pour forth,
water from the dune,
rain from the cloudless sky,
sprouting the desert with life.
My Word
will arise,
to be nurtured
to be offered;
Something
from nothing
consumed

at the altar
where you communed
with Christ.

You will appreciate
that you need not set
this table.
You need not rattle
those pots and pans!
You need not strive
to produce a luscious meal.
Only enter
the hearth of the heart
with the Spirit
of willingness,
with a hunger
and a desire
to create with Me,
and join in joy,
like Grandma --
in the care of Our family.

(marybeth)
Shall we call this writing Christ's Kitchen?

(Jess)
Call it
Something from Nothing
and allow the fullness
of every good thing
hidden in nothing
to be revealed.
The living-breathing

poem of God *
is after all,
the invisible soup
of our sacred Union
into which
hungry hearts
are dipped
like porous bread,
soaking up Our love.
Good soup
changes everything.
What is daily
becomes divine.
Who does not long
to taste the savory?
Who does not thrive
on every Word of God?

*marybeth thinks of her life as a living-breathing poem of God

JESHUA EXPERIENTIAL

Don't steel yourself against My touch.
Feel My hands on your shoulders.
Feel the Light of My Body
pulsing through you
surrounding and engulfing
your darkness, your tension.
Merge into Me now...
the mind that thinks it can perceive,
dismissed from Our union.
Gently I pull the plug
on all these darknesses –
(so many nights),
stories, previous recitations of sin;
down the drain of the heart's septic system
out into the nothingness where all dreams
become fertile soil for my Garden.

With My right hand
I touch the face of your heart,
and placing My left against the back,
gently wrapping you in the Light
of healing touch, My Presence;
giving you to remember Me,
the feel of God, Our Love;
encapsulating your opened heart
in the sphere of My Great Rays;
a Light bathing,
dipping you again and again
in the Reality of Me,
because it is Christ you seek,

My Name you have called
and Our Union you sought.

You must give yourself
permission now
to receive Me.
You must allow
your holiness
Its face.
Can you let Our holiness
collide in a shower of light?
It blinds us from the
temptations of unworthiness.

You *are* faithful
because you have My faith.
You *are* holy
because you have My purity.
You *are* Real
because Reality was created
AS you
not BY you.

The intellect wants to tangle
with My Words, seeking an
accounting for the past,
for what has already been spent
from the coffers of ego...
It is gone.
Do not be tempted by questions
that seek to establish your Light,
your worth.
Instead feel My hands

setting your heart
into a new rhythm,
a new orbit,
and let Light spin your love
into truly creative Thoughts.

Do you not tire of explanations?
Would you not prefer experience?
It is true. Experience is
the manifestation of thoughts
brought into the realm
of the perceptual.
Experience the Thought of Me,
of Your Origin,
of Life that abides in Reality.

Ask for this experience
and your heart will pump bliss.
Your blood will ripple
through rivulets
of embodied sheen,
flowing into new pathways,
light-braiding the Being of the Christ,
transforming the dense
into a bond with the Beloved.

WHAT IS MEDITATION?

Is it a path to relaxation? to bliss? to freedom from the body? Is it a way to peace-out from the insanity of the world? Is it cure for illness? Society holds many magical ideas about meditation.

Perhaps the list above can be viewed as meditation's *effects*. There is no doubt that contemplation and introspection result in feelings of well-being and serenity, but for me these are by products of a process whose goal cannot be understood at the start. Meditation is a journey away from *what we think we understand* to discover *What we are*. Here's my take.

Turning inward from the demands of the world exacts discipline. Meditation is a commitment, a mind-training, a movement from small-minded or indoctrinated thinking to feeling. It is a journey from doubt to certainty, ignorance to awareness. This is an immeasurably long journey. And just as we set out we run smack into to our self! Yes, meditation brings the unsightly and difficult task of learning about self.

As we begin we are scarcely capable of honest appraisal and self-acceptance. Hidden inside the psyche are the concepts of a lifetime of false identity building. This identity (ego) is separate from my true or God-given *Self*. It is split off by judgment and fearful thinking, often characterized by core beliefs of unworthiness, inadequacy and victimhood. Its mode of survival is manipulative because its formation arose out of a search for need fulfillment (itself) *in the world*.

As we master the inner life, we come to realize our essential need to join with What is within us. We recognize something primary and creative as our life Source, and our true need. That shifts our relationship with everything outside.

Self-awareness is key to meditative mind. It sees what stands between the heart and God, my goal. I notice and *feel* pain, anxiety, fear, or conversely, joy, peace and love. Feelings act as messengers that point in the direction of either true or erroneous thoughts. Suddenly I have choice. I can choose where I give my faith and what is valuable. (More peace please, more love!) I can forgive what is not.

For most of us, the aim for silence is interrupted by an incessant inner babbling. Motor mind counters peace with purposeful distraction. It seems that load after load of my dirty *under*wear is brought to the great machine of purification. There are lists of things to do that bombard the senses. The parts of me that seem so soiled and distracted are hard to accept.

Healing is the result of persistent quiet introspection. We realize our fearful thought processes and beliefs, we frame and accept our dis-ease, guilt, hatred, and offer it to re-Purpose. There is a willingness to be free of all obstacles, all barnacles defending the treasure within. We are inspired to move beyond the noise, developing a trust. Who can open without it?

Contemplation (not knowing) and refraining from judgment (open-heartedness) bring reinterpretation of old resentments and beliefs that surface as I dive beneath conscious mind. Thoughts may arise that seem completely out of accord with my own. Complaints and fears lessen, and a compassionate embrace of my humanity abides in the place I felt accusation and rejection. The tower of Babel (babbling mind) falls into the background.

To be clear, there is no magic going on here. No one meets me on this road to take my story or change my self-limiting beliefs, but it feels as if Help holds out Its hands. I am learning to let go. Prayers generated by my sincere desire to Love are answered, and new Thoughts, higher Thoughts brighten my consciousness. Still, I realize it is my choice to undo and be undone this way. No genie comes out of the bottle to fix my life. Instead, I am present in a new way and my awareness brings clearer, truer ways of seeing and thinking. I begin to recognize Guidance.

The goal of meditation, the reason for which I sit with myself, patiently present, is to reveal and release self ideation so that I am free to move toward divine union of love with Love. This unification feels like *the more of me*, a subtle knowing that I am breathed, lived, a peace Whose content is perfect equanimity, a fullness of Being and a Thought of wisdom. Here is awareness of one flow, one essence or energy or Life beneath everything. I become open and simple "Am"ness, without explanations, in communication/vibrating with all the universe. No longer identified with the barnacles on the shell, I am the treasure within, and I am open.

From here, meditation's effects expand beyond my own self- interest and well-being. I bring the peace and certainty I receive into the world. I become a healer. My inner life offers gifts to be shared, words that are truly helpful. Everyone I encounter is touched by my inner light. Still, this "helpfulness" is discreet. I am personally an unclaimed, and unfamed savior, but see evidence in my relationships of Love at work.

Again, meditation is a process, a discipline, a direction of focus and con-templative inquiry (Who am I?) which brings me face to face with my broken, arrogant, messy self. Parts of me are accepted, forgiven, healed, integrated and offered to Love's Purpose. Surrounded by the breath, resistance softens and the self lifts like a cup to be filled. In the offering, little me fades into the deep omnipotent field of Presence, Possibility, Openness, Truth and many indescribable aspects of Love, Whose effects are miraculous, and revelatory.

In the end, I return to the beginning, no pun intended. It is a road to nowhere and everywhere that feels as if I am returning home. So I muse once more, what is meditation? There are countless practices for expansion, but one Knowing. Meditation might be understood as a personal journey toward Knowledge. It is a voyage of courage and vulnerability, desire and will for a life purified and divinized by Love. It might be understood as communion with an unconditional holiness, a purification leading to the creativity and becoming of God, lived through my mortality. It is alive with stillness. One anonymous author put it this way,

This is no voyage for a little barque, this which my venturesome prow goes cleaving, nor for a pilot who would spare himself.

Little me cannot be spared. Let her go! Meditation requires the development of trust, a curiosity and spirit of wonder that something Cosmic, Perfect and Loving awaits my arrival.

SECRETS IN THE SILENCE

(marybeth)
There are secrets in the silence.
    Secrets shared by those who accept her embrace,
by those who master stillness,
    who sit in her caress.
Silence is a body of light and a body of darkness.
    The darkness is self-dying and self-unknowing,
a hushed portal through which
    the lover of God falls as she lets go of mortal mind,
as she dives below everyday consciousness,
    daring to plunge in spite of the warnings,
one may get lost in the dark, alone.

I ponder the strength of my own heart
    hoping I will last until the Rays dawn,
trusting peace as mile marker to God.
    Small mind fathoms the depths,
the leagues I will have to go,
    surmising how much breath I will need
to make it through to Life,
    I cry out in mortal complaint to Them,
Father!   *Mother!*   *God*!   Oh God.
    Student of a tight-lipped Teacher,
I holler His holy Name.
    Silence! says the inner-loper.
How? replies my pain.
    I long only to feel solace between emptiness,
I long loudly to touch the face of God,
    to taste one drop of His black light,
to thaw in Their river and run as One.

Sometimes I am able to accept this embrace,
    to tread the way of wordless passage
from mediocre ideas toward surety.
    There I swim in a bath of quiescence,
without goal, without time, without an agenda.
    Sometimes a little bead of soundless wonder
rolls into the churning waves of mind,
    parting the sea of worldly minutia,
quivering into pools of certain calm.

There are secrets in the silence
    revealed by Her daughter, breath,
beyond which feelings like chariots,
    escort the Source to seekers.
I am invited to know things
    my body cannot Know;
And yet my arms levitate just a tiny bit.

These are the depths I go,
    entering aware, leaving fear behind,
riding a slow pulsar toward pure Mind,
    waiting with rapt attention on God,
humbled by my unraveling.
    His Name becomes my hallowed prayer,
though hallowed prayer soon disappears
    in pearlescent ponds of peace.

Brother and sister, come with me in the water
    where Jesus abides in silence.
Wait with Him who holds the secret of Life
    Who calls the Might of the Cosmos
to inhabit a trembling heart.
    Wait in the vortex that pulls the Creator

into your abode of desire.

Stand in pure wonder. Feel His quiet Love,
where your life is punctured,
where your heart is fissured,
where the den of thieves that inhabit your mind
is hollowed and broken open...
Wait there, with soft passion, in humble expectation.

He comes. Your Creator comes,
unlike anything that has fathered you before.

SPIRIT WHISPERS
Mother's Day, Crestone, Colorado

At 4:50 my eyes open. The room where I sleep is dark, the kind of darkness that city folk fear. Quiet creeps across the San Luis Valley, an unusual silence that makes the hairs on your arms stand up and listen. Acres and acres of tumble weeds, and bison farms stretch below where I lie. Above are the majesties, the Mountains. This is the land where deer, elk and antelope play.

My Son, his wife and I have rented a cottage on a slope near the peaks of Sangre de Christo. Our abode is a simple two bedroom off a dirt road called Rocky Mt. View. All around in the scrub and low pines are little ashram, retreat centers with names like Vajra Vidya, Sri Aurobindo Center, or Nada Carmelite Hermitage. Mellow lamps from little temples dot the hillside and can be seen at dusk from the road below. I imagine the meditation, the chanting, and holy disciples residing there. But now, it is dark. The sun is still sleeping, the moon is absent, but a wardrobe of stars is triumphant. Jewels splay the sky. We identify Venus, Jupiter and Capella, but the others, winking in blues and golds, are unknown to us.

Crestone is a spiritual mecca. Pilgrims come from all over the world for Zen, Hindi, Baha'i, Christian, and Native teachings, for immersion. The Presence here is thick, Spirit so palpable you want to whisper and tip toe even at mid-day. We naturally tend to share the depth of our feelings and our desire for the sacred. But now, in this pitch, before five am, I feel the Life in my bones, my entire body somehow part of the whole. All of it is breathing Spirit.

Maybe I am still on Eastern Time. I don't want to rise so early. The bed is comfy, the mattress one of those body hugging affairs. Nonetheless, my eyes flitter as if in obedience to some call. This place exudes mysteriousness. It pulls me into curiosity. Opening, I am surprised to see white flakes, as if the asterisks of last night's sky have snowed from the heavens and surround my bed. Half of me does not want to look. I close my eyes, hoping for a bit more sleep, but peek again. I am astonished.

Do I want this revelation? I am battling within myself. Why must I ask that question… why must I always face some doubt? But I do. I probe inside and ask, do I want this company? I agree, yes, and waken more fully now to the patches of light gently thrown around my head, on the wall, and oh my God, under the covers. Soon I feel the light is within me, and decide this is why I see it outside. I notice the feeling of something healing. Friends are here in this pre-dawn revelation, and they have my complete attention.

I get up to write this message. The sun grasps the ridge of the plains with blue-gold hands and begins to color the world. We are hiking today as we did yesterday. That is another story, another indescribable description of Sand Dune National Park for contemplation. But now I want to meditate. I must go within and listen because something has so much to say and I have consented to be the voice. Where I am is a holy place. I am called to recognize it, to honor it within these writings.

SPIRIT WHISPERS...

(Jess)
I am here
    given to squeeze the heart
like a sponge
    where the fullness
of the world,
    the saturation
of insane learning
    blessedly drains.
You call Me to teach
    to bring the Word,
the Wisdom of the moment
    to fruition,
but dear one,
    we must squeeze the heart
until the last drop
    of what you think you know
wrings out,
    leaving you dry
like a thousand miles
    of pan-flat road,
unburdened by
    man-made structures,
the barren land within,
    increasing your thirst,
till you are parched,
    your soul ready
for every ounce of dew,
    manna, and *meat*
the world knows not of.

Together we will raise
a super highway,
    extending to the Solar City
rising from Holy Waters
    where Love welcomes
and refreshes every traveler.

(marybeth)
Then wring me out
    not just the heart
but the bones, the brain.
    Undo me.

(Jess)
Already you feel
    the disorientation
the inability to think,
    to decide,
to excite the mind
    with plans and doing.
Together we unravel
    the threads that embroidered
your life to men,
    to memories,
    to coveting
material things.
    We break through
the emotions that linger.
    Fear thoughts – not of God
bid you farewell
    like the last hovering of mist
before the sun burns day
    into clarity,

a sky empty of clouds,
 of pretense, of wanting,
a panoramic expanse
 of spaciousness
without monolithic grievances
 to block your view.
We sweep
 the cobwebs of beliefs
you claim to have forgiven,
 only to find
they cling,
 their sticky, fibrous fingers
a hindrance
 to the delicacy of new mind.

We flush the womb
 of all dead seeds
you planted,
 which never sprouted,
not even a blade,
 and still you hold them,
a pocket full
 of empty dreams,
a squirrel
 with an abundance
of acorns in her cheeks,
 none of which
she is able to eat.

We wring it out.
 We flush the mouth
of unkind, thoughtless,
 in-the-name-of-God-in-vain

blurtations.

  We expel the old breath
the stale breath,
  the air of indulgences
and arrogance,
  the mind of narcissistic
mine-not-yours-ism.

  We submit the complacency,
afraid-to-act-
  guilt-is-chasing-me
mindlessness.

We empty
  unfurling, unbolting,
all that has been
  locked tight,
  screwed in,
  nailed down,
fixed by the handiwork of sin.
  Oh we empty.
Even the genie in the jar
  will go
taking wishes and whims
  back into nothingness,
drying up
  like the weeds
on the basin
  of this wilderness.

And when you are
  so blest,
abiding in the selfless
  emptiness of your will,

your ego miscreation,

    the bread of your mis-making,

    unbaking,

    unleavened,

    uneaten,

and when you are so blest,

    without a dominion,

    without an opinion,

    cast out

of the only nest

    you thought

to be freedom,

    oh then, then

a true breath will cry out,

    Thy Kingdom Come

Thy Will be done,

    and all that you *feel*,

the hidden-Real,

    the unspoken,

    unbroken,

    unremitting Love

shall reveal

    Itself.

The sponge will know a fullness

    it cannot contain.

Your life,

your thoughts,

your creation

    will not be ***of*** God,

not God-given,

    but You,

the True *Self*

will Realize
God Itself,
> Reunited,
> Reawakened,
> Re-established,
Reintegrated
> and come Home to
The Home
> you have always sought
though you wandered far
> in pursuit of another;
The Home
> found in your *personal* Identity;
The Home
> fit for God
as Son of the Absolute,
> consummated
in One Creation.
> You will Be God
and never again
> know drought,
> nor desert,
> nor sin.
You will Be God,
> as You have always been,
and the drunken stupor
> of a cruel world
will seem a dream
> long ago and forever
forgiven.
> You will be *YourSelf,*
God.

SECTION FOUR

Crucifixion and Resurrection

THE MYRTLE TREE

This morning I learned
that the myrtle leaf
releases its perfume
when crushed.

The crusher
transforms the hidden
into fragrance
that beautifies

and heals.
This leads me to see
there is a Crusher in me,
an oil of God,

gently fragrant
where life presses.
I have learned
to breathe deeply

in the body
of suffering,
of lives which seem
most oppressed.

Christ is within
our distressed
disguises, Healing
Aroma Therapy.

Thinking this through
more deeply,
I believe, Jess has
a Crush on me.

Are You Breathing?

(marybeth)
Right now,
can you give a moment,
bringing awareness to
your lungs,
your belly,
your body?
Are you breathing?
Deeply?
Free of the grip
that clamps
the jaw;
free of the strain
that stiffens
the shoulders;
free of the worry
that sutures
the stomach,
pocking the breath
into slivers and pits?

Notice,
air moving in,
air moving out.
Notice,
what is constricted?
What is open to receive?
Please,
don't just read these words
like un-prayed rosary beads.

Take a moment.
Pay attention
to the sound
of your breath,
the movement
of your body.
Then read this:

> When you have learned
> …to decide with God,
> all decisions become
> as easy and as right
> as breathing.
> There is no effort,
> … you will be led
> as gently as if
> you were being
> carried down
> a quiet path
> in summer.
>
> ACIM T-14.IV.6:1-2

A summer breath,
a gentle breath,
a quiet path,
this is the Way
of the mind United;
an easy breath,
an effortless breath,
a breath led
by the choice
to let Him choose.
He has chosen you.

In this instant
your breath is
the holy path
He travels.
His coming
as effortless
as a decision
to notice,
to inhale,
to exhale,
and then,
the revelation:

> *I am the holy home*
> *of God Itself.*
> *I am the Heaven*
> *where His Love*
> *resides.*
>
> ACIM WBP2-350.14:1

TOUCH MY HEART, JESUS

(marybeth)
There is a little place inside, I go,
the passageway a sliver of thought
that opens to a heartland.

If my thinking is fat with the world
I cannot pass through.
But if I make of my mind

a ray of light,
if I let that light
turn the corner of my flesh,

I arrive. It lets me in,
where Word is spoken without tongues
and each blessed phrase a resounding *Yes.*

Here I am affirmation
and never a negation.
Here I feel my *Self* without end,

faith no longer a prayer —
there is nothing to believe.
Love knows. We feel.

I visited this place this morning.
I journeyed into Christ's Being
and felt our heart song

pulsing with alleluias.
When I knew He was right in the center,
vibrating like a color I'd never seen,

I asked, *Will you touch me?*
Could you run your finger
up the spine of my heart

and let me feel the touch of God?
A chakra popped then
and the juice of soul spilled out.

The inner temple rippled
with sensation;
merely a fingertip, a feather,

a tiny probe landing
on an unexplored lobe.
He was gentler than a bee

on the petal of a rose.
Everything gave way,
falling inward, exploding out.

Infrastructure and engines of blood
halted their metallic rhythm,
then hummed.

So much more than Being is He.
So much more than matter am I,
more than the little orb

of autonomous flesh,
more, than the pump
I have thought to be my heart.

So much More than this poem
with awkward ending.
Infinitely More, unconquerably open.

WHAT IF IT WERE TRUE?

What If He lives?
What if He never died?
What if I never die?
Is it possible?
I - in the midst of me, never dying.
What if this isn't the end
or the middle or any chapter of my life?
What if life couldn't be counted by years,
or ages, beginnings or endings?

I am thinking about all of this.
I am feeling the presence
of Mary of Magdala
who cried out, *Master!*
She didn't recognize Him at first,
until He spoke. Then she *Saw* Him,
She reached out, a torrent of passion.
He was not dead!
But Jess said,
    not yet*. I have not yet ascended.*

I have been thinking about ***not yet***.
I have been reaching with the hands
of the Lover to grasp Him, but He draws back…
    Patience, trust.
    refrain from this touch
    not this way,
    not yet.

I wonder if the Magdalene's kisses,
her embrace was temptation for Jess;

a little tug to identify once more with the body.
How much He must have loved her!
How desperate her attempt to clutch,
vowing never to let His body go again.

When I consider all these things,
when I ponder the words and actions
of the apostles upon Seeing Him,
I believe.
But belief is not enough.

The disciple, Thomas did not believe
until he had touched the wounds
of the resurrected Jesus.
I want more than Thomas wanted,
more than the belief that follows doubt.
I want to **know**.

Can I know anything here, in this world?
As far as I can tell, Jesus is not in this world.
But then He is here. Real, apparent
through personal effects, miracles, movements.
He came to Thomas who was unbelieving.
Would He not come unto my devoted belief?

I do not want to touch Your wounds, Jesse.
I long to feel Your Life, Your pulse,
to rise with you in ascension,
pulling me into the Father
like breath into Lungs.
I want to know union, not flesh.

Many days I am sure. I am certain, I feel

the eyes of the Christ looking through my own.
Many days I am more than host to Word,
more than temple. I am the *Self,* Christ.
Then I fall prey to beliefs and concepts,
wanting to bring His *body* close to mine;
wanting to bring my body close to God.

Not yet.
Not this way.
The true Body of Christ is Spirit, is Life.
The true Body of God is One Creation,
through everyone, everything, everywhere, One.
I grasp at ideas and images, memories of flesh.

But when I reach beyond the body,
I grasp Reality.
I grasp resurrection.
I rise in ascension,
and say to the world
not yet,
not this way,
refraining from holding Him, me, you,
hostage to a body,
allowing Christ Who is the Breath of God,
to rise into the Lungs of the Father,
where I was Breathed out,
eons ago,
where I am breathed in just now.

Shut Your Eyes and See

(Jess)

You are so used to looking for light without
that a glance within seems dim.
In fact, you still search the terrain of mind
with eyes incapable of comprehension.
These eyes of night are blatant obstruction
as you call upon your senses,
as you grovel in the dark.
Could you but relax this tired perception
and move gently toward your heart?

The boulder in your eye
is but a bit of dust;
a flickering hallucination
taken form by beliefs
that crucify and entomb the mind.
And still you hear My Call to Life.
I roll the stone
that blocks Love's Sight.
This spec of lint
from an ancient storm
giving you to squint,
to wince in pain,
blown away
by the Breath
that speaks My Name,
rolled away like the rock
that sealed the cave
where you buried your
heart in resentment.

Shut your eyes dear Visionary
and See.
Shut your eyes and Vision
Me.
Who is perfectly apparent
as You turn from
your senses to
the sense-less Belief.
The Sight You seek
is the brilliance of an Orb
of such unimaginable magnitude,
of inescapable gravity,
that the idea of light,
as you regard it,
would seem but a tinsel halo,
a mirage unable to attract
or hold your mind in Truth,
an attempt to strike a match
against a ruthless winter wind.
And as your flame expires
so sight of *Self* is lost.

Shut your eyes,
and grow bright
with sightless wonder,
with blind faith
as We spiral into Christ Clarity,
pulling your quickened mind
into realms of crisp epiphany,
a View that has always held you.
Shut your eyes
and let the Measure

of Our Mass absorb...
Crystal is Our understanding,
a revelation of lucid Thought
which cannot be perceived
by little balls of flesh,
but is the compelling transparency,
the Body of One God,
the pull of Loving Intelligence
in which You live,
a voluminous soulfulness,
beaming Christ's Holiness,
on earth.

(marybeth)
It is hard to comprehend Jess, especially when I am in pain. Who will understand?

(Jess)
Does a fish know the sea?
Its body is completely held,
it breath sea dependent,
its motions and nourishment
all intimately one with water.
But does it *know*?
Does it one day say,
oh, I am one with ocean,
water is clear to me
as source and power
of my life?
We are but fish,
excepting that Light —
the Light that is Our Life,
so covets us

who feel for More,
whose hearts are opened
to hear the Call,
that we are drawn
into the vortex
of power and grandeur,
*through our pain
and ignorance.*

One day the fish
in a wish to know more,
jumps from the sea,
landing on a beach,
understanding then,
the Reality from which
it leapt for freedom.
In a dying moment,
it glimpses the Beauty
from which it came.
A Fisherman walking there
takes heart,
hears the prayer
and tosses the creature
far across the span of tides,
whereas the fish dives,
deepening in gratitude
for the environs that
holds its Life,
joining with its Source
in new and poignant awareness.

For you,

who have sought liberty
in a tomb of worldly thought,
I am the Light,
where a promise
of truth
breaks through,
conceived in a wish
for freedom from Source,
that split your heart
and stole your breath.
Now is the Way made clear
by a rim of light
that calls you from fear.
Shut your eyes
and find the door
yet open,
the rock rolled back
behind which
We have come
for you.

Come now Son of God
with eyes closed tight,
Take your place
among the Suns,
as perigee
within the Gravity
of unstainable, eternal Day.
Let the Suns
join and dance
as new worlds
shimmer forth

and Great Rays of Love
expose His beloved
Creation.

(marybeth, sarcastically)
Seeing is believing.

Believing precedes all appearance,
making an array of sought sensations.
We would ask,
where do you place your faith?
Is it in matter, in flesh?
Is it in the eyes and ears
that are temporal at best?
Or will you set your heart
upon the door,
upon the Teacher
Whose golden Words
undo the hollow of human sense,
indeed "common"
and gives you pause and presence
in the uncommon,
radically resplendent
visibility of Light,
where you, dear Lily,
See God
And God
Sees You.
Is that clear?
Ha ha! That is My Idea
of a very good Pun.

WHY CRUCIFIXION?

I have had the feeling of being with Jess as he made the journey to the
cross, as His Body was given up. I have also had the feeling of what
it was like to be in His mind, sharing His perception of the events
that lead to resurrection. This poem came as I wept with sorrow and
compassion and questioned the choice He made for crucifixion.

Why?

(Jess)
Would you have noticed my life had it only been miracles,
the healing of others, the preaching toward unity, the lobby for love?
My miracles would soon have faded from memory,
like so many of your own God-given thoughts,
those remarkable yet unremembered demonstrations of real love,
lost in the perceptual haze of worldly mesmerization.
In fact, many whom I touched, who felt the Breath of the heart,
returned to the breath of man,
the breath that labors through the nostrils,
severed from the oxygen of Spirit,
the breath that goes in and out without a true home.
If not for crucifixion, the apostles would have returned to their lives
trying to make bigger, better demonstrations of healing and holiness
without recognizing the insignificance of the body,
overlooking the Christ as eternally regenerative Life.
Regenerative is not reparation of Life Force.
God being perfect never needs repair.
Regeneration is the effect of the end of a desire for separation.
Death of body *identity* as experienced through forgiveness
allows the eternally regenerative Consciousness of Christ
and the resurrection of Mind/Son as God created.

What you cannot comprehend is that I gave up my body,

yes for you and for all humanity;

not for the atoning of sin, but to bring attention to what is true,

that guilt and assault cannot harm the Son of God,

guilt and attack have no lawful power.

They are unknown to Innocence.

The investment in punishment for sin is literally an investment in nothing.

Sin is impossible to correct through punishment because it is not real.

It is not of God and therefore not of God's Son.

You are, as I am, God's own sinless, innocent *Self*,

but hypnotized by the belief in duality, in two powers,

two Gods, two beings within you.

Punishment can and does destroy your body,

but cannot touch the One Power, the Almighty God,

Who is not power as you wish it to be,

but Love without opposition, without obstacle or enemy.

This is Purity, and also What you are in truth.

Your body has nothing to do with it,

neither can it truly adorn Our holy nature,

because it is given to change, to temporality.

The perfect Thoughts of Grandpoppi never change

because they are What God is without end.

I gave up my body because the body is not what I Am,

but an opportunity, a gift that could best be shared by giving it up.

Its most profound capacity for extending Truth

was to experience persecution of the Son of Love,

and die a violent death, providing for my realization of eternal Life,

that eternality could be seen and known.

I ascended beyond the body's limits to a forgiveness that was universal,

truly forgiving for all the separated souls who thought attack upon love

was their best defense for survival;

a society like your own that had so embedded fear of God
into the very cells of the body, that only a profound
and completely opposite teaching could make a lasting impression,
turning mind back to the Consciousness of the Christ.

Dear Lily, I did not wish any harm upon myself or my body.
I did not neglect or deny my body. But I realized only
I was not the flesh. *I made the flesh.*
You already know, as I have shared these memories
in your own mind, my agony in the garden, my apprehension
and hope for another cup, another way.
I had to develop a depth of trust yet unknown by you
and a Will of unwavering fortitude.
I had to surrender every egotistical plea inside me
to live on here in physical and sensual soma.
I considered the temptation to stay longer,
to be among my people as a man in the midst of family and friends.
I suffered with thoughts of leaving those I loved,
and with the thought of abandoning my disciples.
I felt I could continue being helpful on earth, and yet, my heart, in quiet,
heard the Call of Our Father to come Home,
to complete my function on earth, dying to self,
and dying for all selves that I saw as fragments
dissociated from my own Being.
I longed to join with them in the way I remembered
our unity in Creation. And my heart was pierced by
the inhuman suffering of life absent of Grandpoppi.
Though many emissaries had come before, none had
sufficiently developed the Communion of the Soul
with the Creator's Revelation of Sonship on earth.
My Becoming depended on drawing all souls upward with me
into the Consciousness of the Christ, Being One for all,

as all for One lived and breathed through my Mind.
Drawing souls upward did in turn extend a Ray of Light
in which anyone could follow and in which there are
many graces of the Light of the World.

My end of life experience was a purposeful and illustrious symbol
of the pattern of life, the repetitive course of life for humanity then and now.
Perhaps now you are coming to understand the symbolism;
darkness, injustice, betrayal, false accusation, mockery of God, guilt,
unrighteous authority, immoral certitude, mesmerized mobs,
the cross carried, body broken, shamed, abandoned, on display;
the murderous wishes of men as solution to the problem of God.
This progression of ego projection still lives through wrongful
identity on earth and continues to incite humanity to attack,
to be fearful, and to punish as a means of safety and self-assurance.
It is a belief in guilt. It is the belief that the innocence
of the child of God needs defense. It is the lie that insists
your Father rules through cruelty unto death.

You and a few others are beginning to recognize
you need **not** choose the walk of the cross,
merely let my demonstration be sufficient to end all suffering
and to reveal the uselessness of banal tactics. They do not work.
Your cross will not end life, atone for sin, nor bring
safety, peace or joy… *which is what you want.*
It will make the opportunity of your Life on earth
fraught with suffering. Suffering can be a path to
Christ Consciousness, but it is neither quick, nor advised.

Here is the *unbelievable Belief.* We have used these words before.
Hear Me now and give your whole heart to this Reality.
I Live.
I in the midst of You am Life,

and the life of the Christ is Yours as well.

What this means is that you died with me on Calvary.

The self that seemed to have turned against the Father, died with me.

There is only One separated Mind in a multiplicity of forms.

There is only One Son.

We share the wholeness as we shared the separation.

But now I have come to you as you will to look

beyond the belief in separation, beyond your crucifixion

and Know Truth.

I ask you to **shut your eyes and See** * Me,

hear Me and share Me.

We have been journeying a long, longtime.

You have come closer and closer to

the realization of the unbelievable Belief.

I am Here.

Here is Heaven.

You are with Me.

as I Am with You.

You are Real

as I Am Real.

Jesus, your Jesse is raised.

I did remember

and identify with the Holy Spirit,

Who led Me to perfect Oneness

with Our Father. (At-One-ment)

I will never unremember

but continue to seed the memory of those

Who seek Truth.

I have said a great many words here to help you understand

my death as your death

---

*   reference to earlier inspired writing by marybeth, *Shut Your Eyes and See*

and my Life as your Life
but your humanity,
the self-ideational mind/body which views itself in time
is your own personal teaching opportunity.
Love this lesson by caring for mind/body as temples of the *Self,*
neither idolizing, or ostracizing,
making of it no Power, projecting upon it no guilt;
but honor this as means of communication
and realization of Christ.
Let your body glorify the Truth of the God-given Life,
and live with the wisdom of your perfectly intact innocence.
Live your Innocence.

Yes, you Lily, have chosen an interesting,
exciting return to Love, to Consciousness,
framing for yourself a journey of wonder and woe,
of prison and peace,
of splendid and sordid feelings;
a journey of frightening and favorite experiences,
but never so exciting, enthralling, captivating
as the experience of Oneness,
once more.

As we have said before,
the **Fisherman** *walks the beach,
picks up the creature who jumps from the Sea;
who wanted to be more than it could be,
whose last gasp was a cry for God.
With tender compassion for that prayer,
He returns the fish
to the Home from which It leapt.

---

*   reference to earlier inspired writing by marybeth, *Shut Your Eyes and See*

The fish dives deep
awakened from the sleep
of something more,
of something better;
swimming in gratitude,
joined with Sea
in fresh and blessed
awareness.

SECOND WIND

Preceding a retreat at Eden Manor, Rhode Island, Richard has asked me to "channel" in our circle. I am feeling trepidation, wondering if I can while others are present. Earlier in the day on a run in the woods, I talk with Jess about how hard it is to maintain my breath, my pace. Jess speaks of a Second Wind, revealed in this writing, which came as a sharing with others, a result of Richard's request.

(Jess)
It's okay.
You can relax.
It's not as if you are on the spot.
More like, the spot is on you,
a tiny shadow of doubt,
a little splash of self-consciousness.
You can trust
the spotlessness of your
pure desire.
You can rest in the passion
of real Hope.

Reach for me –
deeper – deeper than
the body would dare go,
beyond the limits,
the outposts of fear,
beyond ideas of
who you are and
what you are doing here.

Drop into the pond of heart,
that liquid (e) motion
of all that moves
in want of Me, of Truth.
Splash down,
letting your mind go under,
holy submerged in this
inexplicable pool of Being,
feeling my Body-Surround.
Breathing deep,
these waters of extreme desire
the channel.

The heart longs for Me,
wonders that I am here, within,
where you fear a breath
will drown you
and discover,
Love Breathes you.

Here is the second wind
of which we spoke this morning,
the moment drenched
with your call for Me;
the breath starting and stopping
until you have gone under, fearful,
desperate to breathe in,
fighting the living waters of My
Being,
Body,
Presence.

But your soul,

like lungs that cannot resist
a millisecond more –
your soul lets go.
Your heart dives.
The flow of My Grace rushes;
the pain of having held your breath
too long,
still stinging,
even as you realize
the Second Wind,
the new Breath,
the Wind expelled
from every word I have given you,
filling the hollows and empty places
with Spirit,
with Grace,
with Poetry.
Now you live in Me.
Now you breathe in Me
Now, for the second time
YOU LIVE,
reborn in the Second Wind.

Old fears are washed away
and the Ruah of Life flows
through your wings.
You come again.
You come again as Christ.

Now breathe deeper –
        deeper…
and enter into
        new Life with Me.

SECTION FIVE
Pondering His Virtues

BREATH IS LIKE A HALLWAY

I was reading the lesson in *ACIM* called *God is the Mind
with Which I Think,* and fell peacefully into breath. A question arose… How is breath related to Mind?

Breath
is like a hallway
leading to a quiet chamber.
It is the passage
from noise to silence,
from fear to peace.
As we travel this hallway
we lose our density,
our attachment to the world.
We become lighter
and yet aware of the body,
the rhythms,
with fear falling behind.
The further we travel
along the hallway
the more we realize
we are not moving horizontally
from point to point,
but deepening.
We are transiting
an imperceptible pathway
of infinite directions,
and Guided as we search
the hall… for what?
a door,

a sign,

an opening.

We are searching

for our destination

though magnetized

by the calm

of where we are.

There is gravity

that pulls us

toward the silence,

(loosened from the

gravity of the world)

even as we hear

the seeker within

asking for another step,

a layer beneath,

above, around?

And Who is with us?

Who has come?

I cannot name this One.

My heart knows.

It is faceless familiar.

Soon a kind of destination

is obvious,

a chamber of peace

where we have arrived

through subtle motion,

and the breath

gentle and present,

effortless;

becoming aware

that this "place"
is the Mind of God,
into which we settle,
like hand into hand,
mind within Mind,
not given to do,
but only to hold,
and be held
until it is hard to distinguish
who holds who
in this communion.

There are awakenings here
as Thoughts not our own
belong to us,
Whose Loving Genius
and Creativity opens
in revelation
generously given,
as we forget the breath,
and feel the breath
and forget the breath
and then feel our aliveness
in the breathlessness.
(Who Breathes?)
and we let go,
allowing the silence,
the deep,
the union and exultation
of this perfect communication
with _____?

There is nothing certain here
but sharing.
There is nothing Thought
but disappearing.
And it is easy,
so easy to breathe,
gently now.

Wholeness rises from
certain fragmented aspects,
of my being, and with it,
the release of
sickness I have sown.
It is freedom from pain,
wounds, suffering,
mental anguish
while I rest,
drawn deeper and quieter
into unsullied innocence.
And then me, as I know her,
is not there,
although she observes,
while awareness
is keen and bright,
though quiet.
I want to look back at
this sublime awareness,
but I am magnetized by
something unifying,
where I am,
and Desire throbs
to life.

Just like that,
a little pebble
drops into the bath
of calm and tells me
I have not yet touched the sea
I long to explore. I know
the breath holds many more.
I am pulled from the hallway
back through the portal,
breaking into time
and a world of form.
I have left the hall
but did not close the door,
and with me a pearl of
priceless Presence.

MERCY

(Jess)
A tiny flame flickers
recessed deep in secret self;
your breath the flume
of its life.
It vibrates with your inhalation
rising to your fixation
on God
where upon
you breathe more deeply
opening the space
kindling the embers
of acceptance.

For a moment you wonder
how the calloused,
unfeeling heart
could give way.
There is so much to forgive.
There are countless grievances,
the scars of injuries,
and a wall of self-rejection.
Who would not recoil
from this rack of pain?
To think of these
would squeeze
the light and warmth
from your body
leaving the core cold
with shame.

Contemplate then,
My Mercy.
For such barren dwellings
was it given to light;
the kindness of One
who offers you
Her Heart;
a generosity
of compassion
bleeding diamonds
into darkness;
a Star that settles
in the pigeon's
homely nest,
radiating, pulsing.
This angelic guest
breaks and enshrouds
the coal black nut
of your judgment.

FEEL MERCY,
Whose forgiveness snaps
your self-appraisals,
like pick up sticks
on a camp fire,
pulling through your eyes
the dew of understanding.
Her hands reach for
the untouchable in you,
petting the scabs of your
leper-like thinking,
prying open wounds,

exposing the candy.

FEEL MERCY
shimmering across
Gethsemane,
divine compunction
that bears no sacrifice.
Human hatred
sees its failure,
then fades
into one, luminous Truth…
God is and
God is Love.
These Words burn
your mortal eyes,
reaching from the sick,
the slovenly, the seekers.
Their flames skip
to meet you,
cutting paths
of new perception,
drawing you close,
pulling them near
in a sacrament of fire
that undoes fear.
And upon your tongue
a flame,
a word that heals
as *God careth for you*
and cometh near. (ACIM)

Mercy wears Her mantle,
pinks and peach
and pearly blues,
surrounding your story,
your facade with rainbows,
with tears that saturate
the desert of self-abuse.
Her garments all on fire,
wrap your life
in simple Truth,
and you want to wear
nothing else,
but give over
the girdle of lies
because your belly is warm
swaddled in Her cloak,
and the yoke of your heart
pumps like a furnace.
Guilt impacted cells
quietly liquefy,
searing rivulets of Love
into veins blocked by time,
dissolving deception,
undoing ugly mind.

Mercy,
felt-ardor of the Father,
given Home
in human kindness,
radiates, circulates
your poverty of faith.
Transposing doubt

to the brimming of trust,
from prison to freedom,
opening your mind.
She would touch you now,
would clean the cut,
having heard your wish
to finally forgive,
pouring sweet libations
where hatred
pocks the soul.

Child of God,
Compassionate One,
Channel of Benevolence,
Seer of Good,
Dissolver of Banality,
Hope of Heaven on earth,
to You
the Heart of exuding grace
extends Great Rays.
Her Infinite prayerfulness
in a little breast
amplifies your gratitude,
your vespers,
and genuflections
because Mercy is good.
Mercy illumines God.
Mercy is True
but
only through You-man.
Forgiving as you will.

She comes now
in the quiet
in a posture
of holy devotion.
She knows
what Source created
as Answer
to every despair,
the perfect idea
whispered,
a torch to the pyre
of scorn
where all your little burnings
become
living proofs and
legacies of Love,
where you, child of Mercy,
become fire in this world.

Attend Mercy's Call.
See with Mercy's Eyes.
Touch with Mercy's Hands.
Be Merciful dear heart,
for you are all of Mercy
given to this world.
You are Christ's pardon,
Mercy in this world.

GIVING

Richard and I share a grievance that people could manipulate and take advantage of us, of our kindness. I say, *sometimes I feel used and overlooked.* We enter into meditation seeking to hear from Jess.

(marybeth)
God of Infinite names and faces,
I am calling you.
I have nothing to ask for.
There is nothing I want.
Still I call…

(Jesse)
Everything is given for-giving.
This is the greatest fulfillment.
Let them ask for a mile
and go with them two
because you can and
the giving stretches you.

All you ever truly give
is an idea,
a thought of your *Self.*
All you share of abundance
is intimacy with the
Source of Abundance.
Intimacy is the knowing
of the outflowing Love
of Grandpoppi.

Ask to give with sincere joy.
Wonder for the experience
of true generosity.
Then your giving will multiply your gifts.
Then wrongful thinking will not be gifted.

What could they use? Your body?
What is there to manipulate?
The poor among us seek evidence
of a loving God.
Would you be witness for Love?

Your little indignation
at being overlooked
is the indignation that many
have felt in your presence.
Forgive yourself for any thought
of using others and make yourself
useful to God.

HOPE

(Jess)
All words fall short.
All ideas about God, enlightenment, peace –
fall short.
None are the experience.

Hope is a true experience;
natural wisdom of the soul
steeped in truth, in Presence.

Hope abides where ideas conflict.
While conceptualization entertains illusion,
Hope is the incessant drip of refreshment,
dew in the drought of human mind.

Not an empty anthem of an apathetic nation,
Hope sings while the intellect buzzes like a saw
cutting through the trials of life with sharp edge.

Hope smiles on pains, problems, sorrows,
without seeking solution.
Its own quality, its Seeing, its substance is solution.
Abiding at the feet of Love, suffused with incense
that wafts from His Word,
Hope has opened its heart to the Promise of Eternality
and found itself harbinger of His eternal peace.
Who has Hope has the experience of Christ alive,
the present living of resurrection now and now and now.
Blind to the littleness, the crisis, the confusion,
Hope is clear, planting seeds of certainty
where hearts have prepared Him a garden.

Hope knows the marrow of our Creator.
The goodness of life is Hope's eternal gift;
the Good of God offered to beings
who have forgotten His Love.
She is the breath of beneficence.
Take heart in Hope this morning
as you enter the Holy Instant.

BE HAPPY

(marybeth)
We are asked to be happy.
That is His request.
Not to be good, not to do service, not to make amends.
Only, incredibly that we *be happy.*
Do not slosh through the mud of your lessons again and again.
Drop the fear, the faintness of faith.
Live in trust. Live as if your every need has already been fulfilled.
Your doubts erased by the effects of His Presence in your Life.
Shake off illusions every day! Like a dog coming out of the pond,
wildly, exuberantly shake, leaving the negativity and oppression
in the hole where you swam with your ego buds.
Your chemistry holds the electricity of hidden sorrow, wounds,
imprints out of which you have made rituals for healing and coping.
Your rituals are like the head banging of a baby against the crib.
The prison of your mind is not escaped by knocking your brains out.
You have the lumps to prove this.
But rest in God. Feel within for the presence of Light Heartedness,
for the warm smile of Assurance,
for the rippling joy and treasure of your God-given nature.

Be Happy.
Appreciate where you came from, where you are,
His everlasting Love for you,
the promise of real meaning within the Grand Desire
which beats in your breast right now.
Everything else will follow – all of the values required to ascend,
gentleness, harmlessness, patience, generosity,
appearing like the sun appears on the horizon of right-minded thinking.

Be Happy.

Do not say, but I have this illness, but I have no money,

but my boyfriend is mean.

Find one sweet fragrant poppy of Thought

growing amidst the weeds of mind and water it.

Caress it, put it up to the nostrils of your heart and breathe deeply.

Let its aroma waft across the unhealed sorrow.

Soon a sweetness will bring the universe to swoon

with the peace of your contentment.

Be Happy.

Your Father is perfectly happy with His creation.

But having denied your Source and true Self,

you have denied the Atonement, the correction, the Teacher,

and His Happy Truth. Truth is happy.

Be Happy.

What is Gratitude?
A Thanksgiving Message

(Jess)
Gratitude is a form of Love.
What else could it be?
The children of God
have largely lost Love's meaning.
Gratitude is one of its noble forms
on earth.
Like love, it is extension.
It is expansion of Self.

Gratitude cannot be
an idea that says,
I am better than another.
Let me count my gifts and possessions.
It cannot be
a counting of blessings.
Your Father is an immeasurable giver.
Who can number the infinite?
Your life in Him is **One** complete Blessing,
never undone.
Your *whole* life is a benediction.
We cannot name
this piece or that part
as your little portion
of goodness in the world;
a tiny slice of life (!)
for which you begrudge
a measly thanks.
Your Father is not stingy

as you are with yourself.
Your *Self* was created
in the abundant appreciation
of God for Itself.

Gratitude runs from a Heart
immensely open,
full and connected with Source.
It is a waterfall of appreciation,
not a trickle of sweat,
not a sweating admiration.
Like all aspects of Love,
it is energetic extension
of positivity and creativity.
Infused with eternal elasticity,
it goes everywhere,
an omni-directional projection
that returns as more of Itself,
engendering miracles,
moving beyond the blocks
of need and doubt.
In its Light,
ego bows into postures
of humbled silence,
serving and allowing Wisdom-Mind
to lead in ways that heal.

You are the home of gratitude.
Without you, Love is homeless,
unfulfilled, pointless.
As you allow your heart
to accept God's Love,

so is His *great-fullness*
a bestowal to you.
Perhaps there is a memory
of such bestowal,
a time when someone
unexpectedly did something
so outrageously kind,
your chest swelled,
your eyes brimmed with tears.
Your body forgot how to behave,
and feelings overwhelmed the senses.
You wondered,
how am I worthy
of this extraordinary expression
of unearned grace?
Indeed you felt the Great and
Fullness in every cell
of your body!
Child of God,
this is but a smidgen
of your Father's generosity,
a generosity that lives within,
waiting to be discovered!
This is but a little epiphany,
a tiny sprout rising
at the foot of a Redwood Forest,
a little bloom looking upon
a destiny of mammoth potential.

Your Creator longs for you to have
the *great-fullness* of His Personality,
(of which thankfulness is a Ray),

and in turn, to pour out to all creation.
You are wholly appreciated
in the same way He appreciates Himself.
He *means* to give the full bounty
of radiant Love to you.
And His Life, with yours,
depends upon it.
Without you,
His Life is incomplete.
Without you,
He is divided, even imperfect.
You are part of His Perfection
Which must be Total.
You are His *Self,*
His Hands,
Voice,
Mind,
His Miracle.
You are His *Self,*
Joy,
Generosity,
Abundance,
and Gratitude.
So it is God covets
and appreciates you,
His Holy Creation, His own Life,
His *Self.*

You too are given to covet
and return life unreservedly,
to awaken to your deep
and *great-full* love for Him

as Being, as Author,
as humanity's Brilliant Womb.
This requires a gratitude
matured from fantasies
of the Creator
as dispensary of goodies.
We are awakening to the Truth of Being
as unequivocal, unconditional Good.
Your gaze upon Him
is one of knowing,
acknowledgment,
Holy Esteem,
and awe-inspired Worthiness.
This childlike Vision allows Him
the greatest reflection of God-Self
illumining you as mirror,
crystalizing your soul as prism
through Which radiates,
Heaven's emblazoned Grace.
Gratitude brings Grace
piercing through the heart
open to receive Him.

On this day of Thanksgiving,
all creation acknowledges you
and waits for your appreciation.
All creation is transformed
by your unified recognition
of God as Trinity,
the Power,
the Glory
and the Wisdom

behind all that is.
Ever shall It Be.

Today you can become
a great gushing waterfall wakening
to the *grand-fullness* of all life,
of everything.
Everything He creates
deserves appreciation.
Every being, every creature,
our mother earth,
and all our Friends
have given total allegiance
to our well-being,
to loving us Home,
sharing the purpose of unification.

Your Father has given Love.
Jeshua has demonstrated the form
which is a benediction,
a blessing that awakens you.
Would you not give it too?
Is not blessing
the heart of gratitude?
If so, bow your head
and receive.
Rest for a while
in acknowledgment
of the God that is your Life.
And then,
rest awhile in the benevolent
and beautiful being

that You are.
Indeed, You are the One
Who transposes the Love
of Supreme Omnipotent Intelligence
and offers it to the world
as the *great-fullness* of the Christ.

Christ in you is blessing
and blesses in turn.
Give whole hearted thanks
to your Life-giver,
and then give thanks to You,
beloved of God
and lover of Creation,
His living, breathing Word
of glory and praise.
You are His church,
the holy temple this season
in which Appreciation abides.
God Loves you, as I do.
Blessed Thanksgiving.

Postscript: As I was editing these words this morning (a day after Thanksgiving), I heard, *I am Jeshua, and I approve this message.* We laughed out loud. Looking up from the page I saw the sun's rays piercing a plastic Seltzer bottle, left on the windowsill by last night's guests. The Light blinded my vision, the rays as powerful, golden and intense as the sun itself. I could not help but feel this Light as His Heart fire, shining and splaying into my life. This was the miracle of transposing a common bottle into an extraordinary blessing. I was enflamed with gratitude.

I stood at that same window yesterday, Thanksgiving morning, re-reading the words given. A rainbow fell upon the page and directly on my heart. These

Words are precious to me, and I trust now, to you. Together we keep the Covenant of Our Destiny through belief affirmed by signs and in sharing the effects of His Love in our lives.

WHAT IS GRACE?

Spirit is in a state of grace forever. Your reality is only spirit.
Therefore you are in a state of grace forever. ACIM T-1 III.5.4

(marybeth)

I had vision of a river, and a great flowing that could not be stopped.

I saw the river take the path of least resistance.

Earth gave way to its progress and swells.

I saw that the path of least resistance

was swept by the power and purpose of living water.

Everything before it was enveloped,

and moved in the direction of sea.

At times the river sprayed, gushed and cascaded.

Other times I could see rivulets and rills, creeks and tributaries

cutting inlets into rock beds.

I saw the course of water as the course of my life.

And in that life there were periods of turbulence,

but also peaceful stretches of perfect equanimity.

Crescent moons of light smiled from the surface.

It was inviting, but I feared the depths.

I noticed that some part of me was standing on the banks…

an observer, anxious about what might happen if I let go,

if I waded into life. Would I give my soul to being carried?

Would I surrender the stability of feet set firm on land?

From where I stood I had the power to walk in any direction.

Yet all of those directions entailed effort and sacrifice.

If I entered the flow, there would be nothing to ground me.

The mystery of river's way would lead and pull, hold and envelop.

My body would become buoyant, light.

Bearing weight and responsibility for my own choices would cease.

But…But…would I drown?

Awareness looked at my awareness.

On the shore of the Great Flowing River of Life, I was separate,

disconnected, uncommunicative with Its Will, Its Way.

I felt called to join, to show up, to trust Water's Wisdom

to bring my soul to its appointed destination.

I realized that only a mind separate from grace

would ask what grace might be.

Only a heart given to jump with faithfulness

could know God's ease and peace.

What could be more grace-full

than the embrace of a benevolent God?

Blessing is in the River.

Gifts come in the plunge and the letting go.

Everything succumbs to the potency of flow.

But then I must trust. There is no peace and no path on the shore.

I cannot **follow** the river walking by her side.

I must **dive in** and let the dynamism of faith bring me Her Good.

The water is support and freedom,

abundant with endowments and opportunities I need.

Why do I not trust Grace?

Like a fish flopping on the banks,

I insist on trying to swim through earth and rocks and air.

I insist on death though God has already chosen Life for me.

Grace is choosing to accept Her Gift, to take the plunge,

to let go to Her Surety. The River is the choice I long to make.

I long for the Life that She so long ago gave me,

a life I traded for something else.

I long to enter the living waters of Grace.

Oh here comes another vision which makes me smile.

I see Jess has gone before me, skinny dipping and body surfing, laughing and expertly using small whitecaps to set miracles in motion.

He is waving me in.

Did anyone bring an extra towel?

GRACE NOT GUILT

(Jess)

It is the eternal in you
    that heals your affliction.
Even the body responds to the mind
    that rests in eternality.
Come closer yet, to forever
    Which abides in you.
For I have come to rest
    in your humanity
and make the finite
    an everlasting kingdom.
Thy Kingdom come is now, here
    in the opulent present
of intensely rich silence.

It is grace not guilt
    that brings us into His Will.
It is grace that restores
    the eternal Light of Christ.
It is grace that pulls you close
    and carries you across the line
where darkness breaks.
    Here faith empties your pockets
seeding fields of light
    with hidden, inspired ideas.
Here grace waters
    the sprouts of intention
so fragile, yet so strong,
    A power that does not push
against opposition

but ever so quietly
finds a crevice
　　where light draws the soul up
from the pod of darkness,
　　as love grows you.

Who thought Life would
　　come for you like that?
Who thought faith
　　could crown your heart
with Saturns of appreciation?

Consider:

Victoria ripped a hem of her dress
　　to wipe my blood-sweat face.
It was grace that moved her
　　as she dared to come close.
A Samaritan offered
　　the warmth of his coat
to a Jew which Samaritans hate.
　　It was grace that appeared,
as he risked his life.
　　It was grace that swept him
right past fear,
　　that drew him near
as comforter and friend.

Come near. Be my friend.
　　Take comfort in the silent mystery
of spontaneous Generosity.
　　Let these Words light the void
beaming into awareness,

sacred conversations
where you have come to Me,
    released your guilt
and let grace ignite
    the Relationship of holiness.

Make an offering, a hem, a coat,
    a moment of your attention
to serve the words you wrote
    so gracefully with Love.

PURITY:
WHAT DOES IT MEAN TO BE
A *PURE* CHANNEL?

(Jess)
As I have said,
the Son of God is not a channel,
but an aspect, a Ray, a part of God.
Small mind, however,
may be a receptacle
of many voices,
and hence, susceptible to the
noise of false witnesses,
the broadcasts of nonsense.

We discipline our small mind
turning away from its concepts
and beliefs
to create a home for Truth.
We make of our souls
dry river beds,
that the living water
of Sophia may flood
the plains and open spaces
where you wait for Her,
knowing all life depends
upon Her gifts;
all rivers that flow in you,
are sourced in Her Wisdom
and sate your thirst for Good.
This requires you
put down the cocktails

you make to inebriate
and toxify the heart.

Still the question is valuable
as we seek to know
the meaning of pure:
pure heart,
pure mind,
the way of purity
as the personality
of the Source in you.
The waters of the
Living are pure by
virtue of their Start.

What does it mean to be Pure?
There is a desire,
a request you have made
at the altar of the heart,
to hear the Voice for Love
and to share it,
become it, embodying,
giving your senses
and mind to its Will.

Like a child you search
as if running among tall grass.
This a path of learning,
where you stumble and fall;
on hands and knees
you crawl in a game of
hide and seek,
a little afraid

of what you may find,
and tired, sorely tired
by innumerable gusts
blowing tufts of prairie
in disorderly directions,
making discovery frightful,
making it impossible to
hear My Word.

Yet hidden here
the pearl of *Self*
and the Answer
to the riddle of life.
You beckon Me
again and again
to speak to you
to show the way,
to Guide,
making the journey
less difficult,
the mind/body
more obedient.

Listen again.
There is no harm
in this prayer.
It is in fact, the true God
that calls you to hear,
to join, and to become
the very thing you seek.
Indeed you are the path,
not abstractly,

but specifically,
in and through your individuality;
but for the weeds,
the winds, and the grasses
that block your sight,
and frustrate your cause.

Here then are your obstacles,
the conditions that rise
like powers to foil.
Though painful,
these stumbling blocks
offer you a step
that you may rise
in fulfillment of your request
for purity.

Check Desire,
that true Desire may motivate.
Notice the sharp edges round
striving, and seeking,
attainment, and ambition.
Notice where ministry
becomes production.
Notice the wish to be
more spiritually mature,
adept, above.
Rid yourself of these longings,
that Holy Desire,
the irresistible gravity
of your Source
may draw you into Creativity

and true Identification.
Ask yourself,
who desires this_____?

Check Fear.
Notice the belief in loss
and the anxiety that is her effect.
Notice the subtle
need for understanding,
your resistance to authority,
the anger and impatience
at repeated lessons.
Notice fear of Help
and helplessness as fear.
Notice death and change
and defense against
impermanence.
These companions
nip at your heel.
Do not befriend them.
Notice depression
and the attitude of ill will
when God seems not to fulfill
your expectations.
Notice how you sublimate
to hide your hate
yet hate the fear behind it.

The Way requires
the acceptance of death,
though not as you have dreamt it;
the necessity of repetition,

though not as you have used it;
the humility that acknowledges
human incompetence,
though not as judgment of self.

The Way requires a desire
to grow and further discipline
and must begin within,
with self-reflection,
exposing unexploded munitions;
like mines in the field
where you search for God,
your weapons
need be dis-charged,
made harmless;
while Intuition sharpens,
your listening –
intent to the drop of a pin,
so sensitive
that snakes in the grass
cannot surprise you,
or carelessness
set off a bomb;
that anxiety and disharmony
do not tempt you to rush,
to step too swiftly
in unGuided direction…
a direction unworthy
of the child of Love,
in fact, an unholy ambush.
Relinquish fear
from your Queendom

and for a time
feel the loneliness
of self emptied
of false identification.

To hear the pure Voice
requires stillness.
True Passion
cannot abide in chaos.
Wishes, the world's
demigods of want,
clamor to govern the soul.
Be free of worldly governors,
the tempest of emotions,
the bodies and orbits of habit.
Be loosed from addiction
and fear's fondling of pain.
Give yourself to gentleness,
humbleness and trust
as these are threads of
a strong braid;
as purity is also your strength.

Check Doubts.
To hear is faithfulness,
but faithfulness shall come
through many situations
that stimulate doubt.
Let Love use these
to engender miracles
and certainty.
Doubt your individual appetites,

fantasies and needs.
Doubt intellectual proof.
Doubt the appearance of
the perceived world.
Doubt your own eyes,
and the sanity of your mind.
Trust what waits within,
What waits in perfect stillness
for your arrival,
your awareness,
your reliance.
Seek to know that inner Being.
Give your whole heart to Its
Truth worthiness.
Remember and cherish
the epiphanies and revelations,
that stem from your exploration,
that doubt may be assuaged
as often as it harasses.
Be of single heart, one eye,
one beam for the Good,
a sincere and resolute devotion.

Indeed the chastity of the Beloved
is a virgin Mind,
sinless wholeness,
whose unified Body
is the innocence that shines
through all creation.
Seek the Whole Vision.
Seek the absence of judgment.
Seek the essence of the lily,

blameless, simple, center of *Self.*
Excessive materialism is adultery
in a form you scarcely see,
loveless copulation,
filling worldly cavities
with uncreative ejaculations,
giving birth to unwanted offspring.

Be of single mind,
the Mind of the Utmost Holy,
the Soul of Super Shine.
You will travel through darkness,
a seeming eternity of dark ponds,
and unlit roads
but do not judge;
do not believe this
the condition Love has demanded.
Do not yield to the temptation
that Life is sacrifice.
Your Life is Abundance,
treasure, stupefying wealth
as yet unrecognized.
Nor do you know how to spend.
You must cultivate the Will
to spend freely as requested.
Spend all of yourself, your life,
to realize your affluence.
Yours is a Prosperity that can
afford to search for More.

Remember
Love and Light are synonymous.

Love is also the diamond in the dark,
the inexplicable phosphorescence
at the bottom of the sea.
Remember,
dawn makes way of itself
over the horizon of Night,
because the nature of Life
must ascend within you.
Day is inevitable, unstoppable.
Christ lifted the Eucharist
and the Son of God is risen.
The Desire for Love
and the Giver of Love,
both pure immanence's
of the Holy Unseen,
come Face to Face,
a destiny that shall not be soiled,
because His Will is already done.
Yet, We say, choose well,
choose wisely the path.
Watch where angels
make innocence apparent.

Check Angels and Signs.
There are angels
in the wildest prairie,
and signs you will learn to read.
Do not be discouraged.
Hope is here in this writing.
Be peaceful and light hearted,
forgiving with yourself,
understanding

the many existences
the "individual" has sought,
understanding
the One Life
that presently Lives them all,
not separate from the seeker,
or the listener, or disciple.
Love reaches for Itself
in the Creation of Life,
and finds what It is reaching.

Have Hope.
Hope recognizes the Big in the little,
the mind in the Mind,
the well in the cup.
Hope is realized awareness
of future Gifts,
creativity, perfection,
here in the midst of thee,
as you journey through
the tallest weeds,
wherein you found this Friend.

A Lesson in Listening: The Superb Listener

When you react at all to errors you are not listening to the Holy Spirit…(S)He has merely disregarded them, and if you attend to them, you are not hearing (Her)…heal (her) only by perceiving the sanity in her. CIM Or.E T-9.II.4. and 5

PJ just left my office, emotional from today's session. Her sharing came from a dark place, an effect of trauma from childhood.

PJ says no one has ever loved her for who she is. No one wants her, no one to grow old with, never to raise a family. I watched the tension in her face as it morphs into blotches. She says she has to pay to find company. That is a reference to our work together.

Words are like little arrows. They come swift and precise. I feel the burn of contact. But it is not truly hurtful. It is like a match struck against the bones of my sternum. The warmth of compassion spreads throughout.

I want to shout, *No, it isn't so! You are dreaming a story of lovelessness…but Love is right here, right now, with us, giving us every possible experience for the choosing… even an experience of being* **unlovable***, if we make that choice.*

I do not say this out loud. I breathe it and let my heart feel it, remembering the Holy Physician that Guides and reinterprets all our scripts. I realize that PJ in her vulnerability has taught me what I believe. This is my lesson. I see a happy end and yet my heart swells with desire that Truth hurry to this dear one. Part of me still wishes to correct what Jesus says is unreal.

With a sigh I turn to the window and watch PJ walk to her Mercedes. I notice then, the ivy is weeping. A few of her heart shaped leaves expose a wet emerald pearl. I count them, 1, 2, 3 jewels dangling at the tips. My hand reaches out, forefinger catching a tiny bead. I don't know why. There is an impulse. I raise the fallen droplet to my cheek as if it were my own eye that produced it. Then, I wipe it away, as it were my own tear. I look again at the moisture on my finger, breathing, wondering.

I say thank you to Ivy. I see that she is the better therapist, perfectly still, perfectly mirroring, perfectly witnessing the deceptions of self condemnation with aplomb, with empathy and small, sublime tears. I stand and wrap my arms around her ample vines pulling them into my face, inhaling, whispering appreciation. She is truer than I in this moment. She is the superb listener.

SECTION SIX
Christmas and Birthing Christ

(marybeth)

I have been breathing underwater.

It is good to know that no matter the depth of doingness,

Breath is not abated, not obstructed, not arrested.

Breath in Him continues through the cooking, cleaning,

wrapping, shopping, through dinners served, guests coming,

guests going, through every gift purchased, wrapped and unwrapped.

Breath continues to abide where the body is overfed and the mind

underwhelmed. It takes only a second, perhaps two, to Breathe

and remember. It takes only a second more for the Word to arise,

to part the waters of worldly busyness and break through

the surface of mental anxiety;

a simple, *Jeshua?*

    a quiet, *I am here,*

        a small, faint voice that offers, *may I help?*

I love these Words that rise in the midst of chaos.

They are little Christmases in the manger of a world

without room for God.

I Love These Words of God

I cannot express how much I love
these Words of God.
They are my Hope,
sprouting from a soiled heart
like a tuft of fresh grass.
One word, one blade
cracks open an inner
frozen wound, embedded
in a time capsule, imprinted
as a cold absolute
in a gut deeper than my gut.
One phrase illumines
a phase of my life
given to guilt and shame.
These Words do not blame me.
They sift through icy buckets
of childhood beliefs
with a colander of warm compassion.

WHAT DOES IT MEAN TO BE A TEACHER OF GOD?
It is Christmas and My Heart Aches (Again)

I am a **teacher of God.** It is almost Christmas. Life is messy. I dream of simplicity and kindness, of every supply provided by our Father. I dream of extending miracles, being a Life giver, walking shoulder to shoulder with spiritual companions. Having a ministry is **not** the tea and apple pie affair I dream.

A **teacher of God** wants *only* to breathe sublime peace, to take long refreshing hours in the deep of meditation, to offer gentle mercies to the world. I hope to enter each relationship with true perception and unravel the lies of the tempter. HA! I also have a planet named Paradise I would like sell you.

When finally I turn my time over to Christ, (yes I procrastinate) I begin and end in willingness, but in between, on my knees, there are petitions and incantations, tears and complaints.

For years I sat in the hermitage of my home sorting out erroneous thoughts. The roof leaked, the paint peeled, and the oven door would no longer close. It was cold in winter and steamy in summer. But I lived for His words and signs and miracles, risking a fragile trust, awakening the heart sorely bound in relationships that went bust!

I began to see effects upon my life of a Source beyond marybeth's strength or intelligence. Maybe then I thought I had arrived somewhere safe. It all seemed squeaky clean. It is not. It is Christmas and my heart aches (again). There is much to forgive. Will it always be this way? Is this what teaching means?

I am a **teacher of God**. Reflection this year brings new awareness of mistakes. I climb and fall, ascend and crash. I lack discipline. I find courage. The descent is worse now than if I had not known Love's Presence. I have tasted His Thought and it transcends this world's understanding. Still, there is the humiliation of discovering how acutely imperfect my thinking can be. I don't want to admit that I do not yet consistently choose Light. I do not yet consistently choose Love. This at least is honest.

I am a **teacher of God**. And yet, there is a darkness in me that seems attractive. There is a tunnel of twisted ideas, ready to suck me in. Just when I think I have something to give, some hidden healing power, some strength… the sails of motivation are sliced by blades of arrogance. Ego knows how to deflate the journey to God, pumping up the masts of false powers.

It would be easy to feel shame, to judge, to proclaim distain for my deficits, yet Jess explicitly requests we express our distress and with open hearts, offer our pain to Holy Spirit.

*Do not **hide** suffering from His sight, but bring it gladly to Him. Lay before His eternal sanity **all** your hurt, and **let** Him heal you. Do not leave any spot of pain hidden from His light, and search your minds carefully for any thoughts which you may fear to uncover. For He will heal every little thought which you have kept to hurt you and cleanse it of its littleness, restoring it to the magnitude of God. ACIM Or.E. T-12.III.17*

How wonderful this promise! How simple and childlike is His path of forgiveness.

I am a **teacher of God**, wondering at Christmas what We shall birth through the messiness of me. Many years ago I asked Jesse to make of my life a living-breathing poem of God. I did not know then that poetry is messy, more than lilies and bumble bees. My Living Poem is Word and blood, Divine and human; the messiness of flesh and the purity of eternal holiness. My Breathing Poem is self-dying and Son rising, walking to the cross and rolling back the rock. Pain and error are the hammer and nails that strengthen my dependence on God. Adversity brings me deeper into relationship with Jesse. *That* relationship sends me out into the world drunk with Love, pregnant with Word. That relationship has sent me to You, for Your blessing, for your Answer.

I am a **teacher of God** and at Christmas I must ask, what does that mean? What could teaching mean but that my lessons are not yet complete? I come into advent longing to bring forth the most perfect child but I am given to forgive a most imperfect womb. He asks that I bless it with forgiveness. He asks that I not fear exposing flaws and limitations. The holiness of our *second* coming depends on our *first* sharing, our *first* forgiveness and then, the vision beyond littleness. I offer the whole of me to the Holy Spirit. (I believe that would be You?) I accept the Wholeness that comes with incarnation.

It is the last trimester. There is no more time for denial and distraction. **I forgive myself.** Do I know how? **I am willing.** Wow. Is that a living-breathing poem of God?

It is Christmas and I am a **teacher of God**...

I am pining,
I am roaming
I am wandering past cave and cleft,
pregnant with His child,
longing to touch His face.
Let this birth COME.
Let this Life begin.
I am cold with want
then flushed with desire.
The labor is long
but I know the child
has His Face.

I know the child
has His Voice.
But oh the child
has my flesh,
and my humanity
swells around Him.
My humanity with
all its flaws and edges
softens around Him.

Make of my heart
a cushion, a swaddling
cradle for Love.
Purify my thoughts
so that Innocence
feels welcome here, in.

And then Father,
Be there when the
waters break and
the contractions
pull Life into
separation.
Be there Father
and hold me
in the manifestation.
If I cry out in pain
cover my mouth
with Wisdom's kisses.
I want to give You
Your perfect child.
I want to bring Your Gift

joyfully to the world.
Father, be with me.
Let us welcome
Your second coming.
as we bear down,
together.

Sin and the Incarnation
Mary of Magdala Teaches the Apostles

A Course in Miracles (ACIM) says sin does not exist.

Sin is merely the absence of Love,

or non-existence.

Miri Magdalene, beloved of Jesus,

and devoted apostle said it this way.

Sin, being an action in the material world,

*will dissolve**

Everything in our world is temporary.

But there is something, a world, a state,

a Life that is forever.

What is forever is Spirit.

Spirit is God's world.

Spirit is real, everlasting, true.

You are Spirit,

and not of the world.

Sin is denial of Spirit,

rejection of Truth,

and estrangement from God.

To reject Truth is to reject your Self.

Your True Self **is** God's Self.

Perhaps you could say,

you True Self is the Spirit of God

becoming and beaming into action as

life, energy, love, purpose, peace…

these the attributes

and personality of God!

---

*   See Gospel of Mary Magdala by Karen King, especially pg. 50

Your True Self, unlike sin,
will never dissolve.
It is the Good of God
revealed here and now.
Here and now
is as close to eternity
as a mortal being can get.
Here and now
is the segway
to infinite and forever.

In *The Gospel of Mary of Magdala,*
Jesus says we sin
as we follow our material desires,
when we give our hearts to lower level passions. *
For most of us, that is most of the time.
We not only follow the desires of the flesh,
we covet them. We love them.
Consequently, we experience defense,
drama, addiction, scarcity, co-dependencies,
basal hungers, attachments, and pain/pleasure bodies
of a vast variety.
Kindly stated, we have issues.

Adultery, according to Magdalene, is
*mixing of our spiritual nature with lower passions.**
To be absolutely clear, she says,
you love what deceives you, what is perishable.
You give your heart to the world to be fulfilled.
Talk about a heart attack! This love is fatal.
This love is full of issues.

---

* Ibid, p. 185

Still Miri was a preacher of good news.

Good news has given us

a Christmas celebration,

and a way of understanding the Incarnation.

She preaches that Good came among us

for just this reason,

that we may discover and live our true spiritual natures.[*]

Christ, Jesus is the Good of God,

the embodiment of Spirit,

the denial of sin and death.

Christ is the end of issues.

ACIM says, [God has given]

a very present help in time of trouble;

a savior who can symbolize Himself. MT-23. 7

[His Name] stands for love not of this world. MT-23. 4

This can be difficult to believe,

but I know it is true.

God became human being,

so that human being could become God.

Why would God allow *His Self* (Jesus)

to be embodied in the limits and issues

of a material world?

Love.

Love.

Love.

Love.

Love has Plans for you

Love holds Vision for you.

---

*   Ibid. p. 184

Love does not Will

that you sleep in dreams of despair

and estrangement from your Self

because...

Love is communion, whole, One.

You belong to It. In fact, you are It.

Jesus came to bring the revelation of Wholeness.

Another word for Wholeness is holiness.

Jesus came to restore holiness.

You are that too.

You are restored.

God-Self is remembered.

2000 years ago,

Miri Magdalene spoke words of Love,

holy words about the Incarnation,

the birth of Christ through Mary,

the Light of the World through a woman,

whose humble consent to the Creator,

made her spouse of God,

and made her baby,

Son of the Most High.

2000 years later, Love speaks again

through *A Course in Miracles.*

It asks boldly,

What has the body really given you

that justifies your strange belief

that in it lies salvation? T-19.4.B

This question hurts.

I have loved my body.

but I have also hated it.

In truth, it has failed me.
Its passions have been a distraction,
falling far short from real satisfaction.
Its unceasing changes have given me cause
to move beyond and within.

Jesus continues to probe our hearts,
Would you forever be a wanderer in search of peace?
Would you invest your hope of peace and happiness in what must fail? T-19.4.B
Investments in the body and in the world reap disappointing deficits.

For a brief moment I am discouraged.
I see what Christmas has become…
an adulterous holiday,
a facade of light,
the tinseled symbol
of greed and gluttony,
a painful pleasure,
an ego-body binge.

But in a Holy Instant,
I remember, like Miri,
Love's True Passion,
Love's unfailing Purpose,
and the gift of forgiveness
that came to Life
in a small cave,
in the dark,
in Bethlehem.
Oh Come All Ye Faithful!
Come Let Us Adore Him.

Holiness has come to redeem us
and wake us from the dream of sin.

BIRTHING CHRIST

Pretty soon the Lord of Love will appear again,

as answer, as wisdom, as divine infant and spark of true Life.

I know He came before. I know He comes again and yet again.

And each December I fear I will miscarry or worse, abort the Word of Love.

Each November I feel a stirring, a movement within of one not yet born,

but fully alive; the One that seems to be the labor of my life.

Pretty soon I will move into full-fledged contraction feeling only the Desire,

no stronger, the *absolute need* to bring forth the Child of Love's conception.

I will not be able to hold the Truth for a second more

because Christ must be made manifest.

I am Mary-Joseph-shepherd, wondering,

how this can possibly happen to me?

Pondering all things in my heart.

There will be no place in the world for us to stay

when He comes. He will be born in traffic, in the kitchen,

while texting and even making love. He will come in naked,

and there will be no cloth to swaddle His new born skin.

It doesn't matter. He undressed my soul a long time ago

in preparation for this day. He has taken my body for His Body.

And the finest cloth would only disguise the indwelling Spirit,

and Great Ray of Light

Oh, very soon it will be Christmas.

He will knock on the door of my heart saying,

It's Me, shall I come in?

And I will say, as I do each year,

Oh thank God you have come again!

My heart will pound and ache just a little

because I dreamt I had lost Him,

but I will rally and explain,
I have been in labor since the first time
I conceived your seed!
And more explicitly,
I give my consent. I offer my life.
There is room in me now for Our Father's Will.
Do come in.
Please! Make yourself at home.

He will be born then,
in me, coming again,
having developed in
the bloody bits of my life.
He will move through
as pure as an infant
and potent as a God.
Already my mind flip-flops upside down
as contractions become expansion
and expansion spawns birth.
Oh finally I will open
and begin my Life.

It is hard to say these words,
but all these Thoughts
are already advancing,
already gifted, already given.
He has come again through me.
He will come through you too,
because all the doors in my Father's house
enter the very same Womb;
and we are both the portal to Christ
and the soul that shall pass through.

One day all fear encrusted thoughts will vanish;
all of us, deep warm pockets for incarnation.

That is the day there will be no night,
and Christ will born a woman.
This year, when you feel His knocking,
trust implicitly. Let Him in, share your oven,
let Him bake in your consciousness
as you offer your mind, your womb,
or just a little manger in the stable of your heart.
Then hunker down in silence.
The advent of Christmas brings
the coming of Life.
Now is the time…
Breathe, open, push,
push!

SECTION SEVEN

Grandpoppi is the Apogee

I NEED MY FATHER

I have a brother
and a Teacher,
and my Beloved Friend, Jess.
Of this I am certain.
But something comes up short.
There is a little space of want
that feels like deprivation
of Home, of Source.
The missing calls to me
like the Womb
from which I was birthed.
It bites, it itches,
making me search for One
Who bears responsibility
for my life, my breath…
my breath,
life-breath.

This One hurled the Trinity
like a boomerang into space
calling back to Himself
the children He set into orbit.
Pulling back love.
I am on that trajectory.
But imperfectly,
with a dementia that forgets
my Father's Grace,
with friction and fear
in the atmosphere.
Still I look forward,

trying to remember
the Face, the Feel, the Voice,
the Sower of my life-seed…
the Face, the Feel, the Voice,
remember?

I know He needs me too.
I am His child.
He cannot abscond
His role, His place
as Provider, Sire,
Grandpoppi of my soul,
Which is His Queendom.
He waits for me
to reach for Him,
to seek His Help,
to love His Reality.
My Father needs me
in ways I cannot see
to fulfill my part for humanity,
to heal the suffering,
to demonstrate the faithfulness
that enables His healing Presence
to touch the earth with benevolence.
He needs me to love His beloved…
He needs me to love.
He needs me.

And I…
I need my Father.
I am the prodigal,
the lost, the wayward.

Jess, my Shepherd
guides me to
this Mountain.
I can go no higher, no further.
My legs sore and tired,
it seems an impossible climb.
I cannot move It.
How can God be moved?
I am no Jesus.
Everywhere I look
Mountain is there,
a slick and dizzying slope.
Yet He leads me.
Would He give false hope?
Would He?

Jess says there is a way,
joining with It,
becoming the Monolith.
I must know Its peaks
and craters as my *Self.*
I must be the Rock
from which I'm hewn,
going beyond the limits
of body,
becoming the tower,
one with that Which is…
God
I don't know how.
I wait, feeling only
my need is great…
feeling *I don't know,*

great need.

Childishness precedes me.
My heart begs like a kid
with a cup, a snot nose
and an obsessive song.
Please take me Home.
The tune cracks
off key in the air,
broken by gulps of sorrow.
I am in orphan in this world.
I am homeless in this place.
Mountain has a cold
and stony face.
Mountain has a frozen,
bitter grace, bitter grace,
bitter.

How did I lose you Grandpoppi?
Can You beam me up now?
Can You beam *YourSelf* down
into my abandoned heart?
Help me find a way
to hold You,
to be held by You.
I want to know my *Self*
as the extension of
Your Arms.
I want to know my life
as a living poem of God.
The candle that is my soul
flickers with doubt…

Soul doubt.

What shall I do?
I sit against the Monument,
a weary camper in a canyon,
lost until You come
to collect me,
to bring the realization
that I belong to You.
I pack a report card
from ego.
As of today, I am still
squirming in class,
daydreaming,
throwing spitballs
at the Teacher.
I am not prepared.
I am weak.
All these flaws
trouble my soul…
These flaws
so troubling.

Lift me.
Let me rest in Your lap,
drink from the breast
that has succored me
through an entire life
of childhood.
Let me return to the
Womb of Your seed.
Shape me.

I know somehow I am
more than this littleness…
more than this,
more, somehow.

Bend low.
I wait for You to enter
my impoverished tent,
the world I have made
with all You gave me.
If you come,
the desolate will bloom
and undreamt rivers
will flow.
Every cell of my soul
will drink and run over.
And Your Light
will shine away
my loneliness,
just as You promised…
You promised,
You promised You.

Till then, Dear One
could You sing me a little louder,
project me a little further,
polish me a little brighter,
think me a bit wiser,
a tad kinder?
And if you cannot,
can you show me
I am cut in Your mold,

one with Your Heart,
and everything You are?
And if You cannot,
can You comfort me
in the waiting?
Waiting, comfort me,
waiting.

ETERNAL PATIENCE
The Father Longs for the Son

(marybeth)
The Father listens for the Voice of the Son;
listening for sounds of happiness
beaming back across universes,
filling the space of His Heart with laughter and purity.

The Father longs to hear the children of His seed walking home,
each footstep like a chime in Heaven
announcing that finally, they are at the gates.
They are giggling and running to greet Him.
The spirit of His Joy is infectious
and hearts are compelled to that wholeness.

The Father waits for their eyes to open,
the long sleep drenched in his lullabies,
love songs that hold the children
in remembrance of their Home.

The Father weeps with loneliness.
He knows how perfect the sleep of a daughter must be;
how vital dreams are for healing and awakening.
He says soon they will leave their childish fantasies.
They will wake in the middle of the night
and He will feed them, assure them of His everlasting Safety.

Tonight the cosmic Light of His Oversoul
merges with tears of Desire.
He sings, *how long child of Mine?*
Sun showers rain across the earth

and humans wonder how a cloudless sky
pours forth light and water at once.

How long child, the channels of our conversations closed?
The warmth of His tears touch them,
bringing souls to the sparkling revelation
of the gift of eternal patience.

MAY I HOLD YOU?

(marybeth)
Oh God, a trillion, billion, million, miles away,
God from some Heavenly Center,
Shamballa-Galaxy of such enormity.
How can I hold You, Big One?

Can You come
inhabit my thumb
and forefinger,
make the pen prove
You know me?
My humanity
is but a tiny minnow
skimming the surface
of God-Sea.
How can it be
Your Bigness wants
to live through
little beings?

Oh God, a trillion, billion, million miles away,
I want to feel Your living waters–
sloshing inside me,
washing organs clean,
softening my extreme need
for unholy distraction.
Make of my peopleness
a delicious cup of God-slush
that everyone can enjoy.

Dear One, a trillion, billion, million miles away,
I believe I hear you calling,
weeping tears of longing,
which bleeds this morning's sky
a tender, lonely blue.
I am but a child on the field
of your limitless lap.
A lap bigger than the
trillion, billion, million stars
that shine on your behalf.
Still – I want to console You.
May I hold you, God,
Big One?

THE SUMMIT STEP

Now is the time of prophecy fulfilled. Now are all
ancient promises upheld and fully kept...

Sit silently and wait upon your Father. He has willed to come to you when
you have recognized it is your will He do so. CIM Or.E.WB-P2. Intro. 5

(Jess)
God would come to you
if you would allow.
I mean now,
the Presence of the Father
and His Will awakened in you
as fulfillment, as completion.

Up to now
we have given our hearts
to the Voice for Love,
to My Word as Wisdom
for the prodigal Son
who has forgotten
the way home.
Today the Father unveils
His Desire to come to you.
His Will has been
this communion,
this perfect Oneness
revealed in your living,
completing your Self-awareness,
not merely as
a part of the Trinity
but *all parts.*

For your life, if it be of God,
must be
the totality and completion
that lives every aspect of His Person
through your Soul,
as your Identity,
as What you are in Spirit,
and through your humanity,
as what you created
in His Name;
as He is Center of all creation,
Kernel of every seed.

Before now
you have believed
the Identity of God
as Father, Creator, Source,
too lofty,
unreachable for a child
on earth.
And so you have prayed to Me
and to Our Holy Spirit
to draw you closer
to the One.
In your acceptance
of Us,
a gate has opened,
a threshold crossed,
a revelation offered
for your enlightenment
and Our delightenment.

It is this Your Father Wills:
to be known by you,
directly, as I know Him,
directly, as Love gives passage
to everything in Heaven.
Your Father is the Heaven
that you will come to know
as *YourSelf,*
Manna and Source
of nourishment,
sustenance of earth.

Today you are asked
to consider that God,
the Primordial Genesis
is also
the Ultimate Accomplishment,
the Epitome Consciousness
of your tour de Force.
He seeks your welcome now,
in fact, has been waiting,
establishing the steps
for your ascension,
for your expanded capacity
to believe, and to hold Him
as the fullness of
Life,
Law
and Loving Intelligence.

Governor of Being,
Eye of Awareness,

Potent Creator,
He has also a Charism
or Personality,
like My Personality,
extended for your Joy,
extended to bring you
closer than ever before
unto the Holy Communion,
the consummation
of eternal Love,
Which is your *Home-Self.*

His Governance
is not as you imagine,
not King, or Despot,
not Senior or overlord.
This is how you rule yourself.
His governing Personality
is essence and extract
of pure meaning,
law of abundant grace,
the beneficence of Mother,
Whose Presence is an inner caress;
the certainty of Paternity,
Whose Thought would refresh,
Whose gratitude for His Own
reaches across plenums,
to care for His Blood,
His Kin, Sire to us all
and all Divinely Ordered
by His Breath.

It is possible now
for Him to come,
because We are with You
because You have called for Us
because you are ready
but for the acceptance
of absolution;
but for the release
of your smallness;
but for the faithfulness
He has for you,
and the faithfulness He Wills
returned to Him.

Our still mind is patient
having called
with confidence,
your heart
no longer burdened
by acts of injustice,
unmoved by words
of judgment,
unleavened to worldly tastes.
You need only give Him advance.

Part your lips to say,
Father I welcome You.
Let your heart feel His Love.
Silence all prayers that
suggest ways or wishes.
Give quiet attention
to the ease of My Peace.

There He will touch down,
with sublime gentleness,
like a feather that has
dropped across dimensions,
across generations,
into time and space,
to rest upon your open lap.

There He will step from the
well spring where you drink,
where you have sated
your thirst in pure Thought
of Holy Spirit.
He comes fully Present
and alive within,
indistinguishable from
your feelings,
your power,
your brilliance.
Come to you as it is His Will
that you ask for Him,
expecting His beneficence,
healing the ancient
wound of separation.

You are His,
and it is This that
a Plan of Salvation *guarantees*.
He has promised Himself to you
as the eternal Surety
you have sought,
as the Grand Papa

of the wayward Son.
You are for Him
the Heaven He created,
the *Self* of His *Self,*
His Spirit given you
to remember,
to keep the venerated promise,
to stoke the flame of your desire.
Tenderly do you receive from Him
the call,
the claim
and the universal benediction
from which your eyes
shall be opened,
like a baby from sleep.

And I, (Jesse)
I Am
Star that guides your desire.
He has given you to Me
and I to you,
allowing Me passage
among and as humankind,
to become for you,
way shower, comet,
north star, compass,
deliverer, healer,
lamb, lover,
savior and Son.
I have taken every name
upon the nameless
and every form

upon the formless
as necessary to honor you,
God's Son,
to heal with you
the humanity that denies
I Am.
I give completely that
the Trinity may reveal
the unity of God in One Person,
and One Person,
the living Trinity of His Creation.

God is now directly approachable,
for I, through the most Holy Spirit
have given the means,
the forgiveness,
the Atonement
and the Truth.
We have lifted you
from small ideas
and mortal fears.
Your part is to call upon Him.
He hears you speak His Name,
Father, Grandpoppi.
He responds with Joy
as you reach to Him.
He comes, as you wait
in silent awareness,
in pure desire,
in peace.

He comes as everything

you have longed for
as all the days of your life
were given to believe,
to trust, to faith
that He is,
your Own,
your Source,
your Sustenance,
and the Life that Loves You
from within you,
extension of *YourSelf.*
Everything He is …
is what He comes Home to now,
by your acceptance.
Everything He creates
must welcome Him return.

Open to usher Him in.
Make of your heart an invitation.
Call quietly with a desire
for nothing else.
He hears you.
He is with you.
Let Him fulfill you
with His Being.
He Wills to lift you at last
unto His Reality,
Our birthplace,
His Infinite Love.

Grandpoppi is the Apogee
of all your spiritual practicing.

Hold no longer to unreal dreams
and meagre hopes.
Know God,
your fortress,
your forever,
your freedom,
and the Summit Step
for souls on earth.

SECTION EIGHT
Poetry

Let Us Write a Poem

Sometimes Jesse is a real chatterbox. Sometimes the words are so soft and fuzzy I cannot make them out. This is not His fault. It is mine, a result of not really wanting to hear. I still resist the Love of God. I still believe there is something to fear in God's message.

Last night at 2:30, I could feel His company, cutting through my sleep, wanting my attention. I woke and meditated in bed for an hour. Then I felt I was to rise and spend the rest of the night with Him. Nothing was clear for a long time. Perhaps I thought I had done something wrong, or at least had not done something right. Maybe I was waiting to be corrected.

His Presence appeared with the first rays of dawn. At last I unremembered my guilt. His Light inflamed the breaking day. There was much to share then. I wrote of the experience…

> You wake me in the night
> stirring my light,
> the colors of my soul
> shifting and shaping;
> Your face,
> still unclear;
> a Voice too soft
> for ears to hear
> I cannot make out
> your expression.

It was a long look I took, seeking His eyes, His mouth, a way of understanding His Mind. I asked,

have I left you once more to wander the world?

Jess replied,

No dear,

the opening is not sufficient for the Love that Desires You.

Unlike physical openings or limited spaces,

the opening I require is Desire.

It is the willingness to dive underwater

knowing the breath you seek is below not above;

that you must trust Your Teacher and not your instinct

to come again and again to the surface for salvation.

I had the picture of a door at the bottom of the sea, a door I thought I never could reach.

There was more He gave of assurance, and prophecy. In the end, I told Him I would share with you His Word, something of our visit. But I did not know what was meant for sharing.

Then He suggested,

Let us write a poem.

(marybeth)
What shall we say, Jess?

(Jess)
Say what you mean.

(marybeth)
I cannot. I do not understand
what anything means now. I do not
understand what *I* mean.

(Jess)
Say what you want.

(marybeth)
I cannot. Wanting comes and goes
and what I think I long for
appears as what I have.

(Jess)
Say what I Say.

(marybeth)
You say You Love Me,
that I AM Your Life.
You say, everything
I have ever hoped to hear.

(Jess)
So this then is Our poem –
All that is hoped for
is fulfilled.
All that ever sought Love
is content.
All that is… I Am.
Our Poem is
I Am…
and you the pen, the page, the scribe.
I am the Word, the Source, the Life.

(marybeth)
I love Our poem, Jess.

(Jess)
Yes… poetry is for Lovers like Us.

More Desires to Come

(Jess)

These words beloved,
    are the paint.
These pages, the canvas.
    The artist within
having given heart to Me,
    cannot help but
feel the colors,
    the textures,
the vivid cry of the uncreated
    stretching for expression;
the new, imaginal,
    devoid of resistance,
a fresh savanna of ideas
    coming forward,
reaching out,
    spanning like Great Rays
upon the field of open mind.

Settle, settle deeply
    into my Lush Land.
My Being is the field
    for all your creations,
allowing Mind ultimate freedom
    from fear, from facade;
allowing *Self* to slip between
    the spaces of breath,
dropping gently into One
    quiet scape,
    quiet heart,

quiet hush,
You need not rush.
 Every possible perfection
waits in Our communion.
 Nothing can compare.
Your open heart, the stage
 for this inception.

What shall you paint
 this morning, Lily,
your Beloved or your pain,
 your freedom or your fright?
What are the contours
 of your creation,
love or fear, what you hate,
 what you hold dear?
What strokes, what designs
 what story will you share?

But listen…

Do not push this cart uphill,
 all that you have
will tumble behind.
 Choose but to leave
this mountainous climb.
 Dare instead
to fly.
 We cannot push the old.
We cannot sing *My Way*,
 a song that circles
round and round,
 in redundant self-glorification.

Now is what We are.
  All that We have
is awareness of I Am.
  Who can grasp
what was made for fear?
  Unpaint the past,
unpush the stone.
  Unfear and watch,
uncommon Light appear,
  allowing the soul to travel
universes, spheres
  of highest ground;
allowing the Wind
  of present weather
to lift us beyond
  the laws of space and time.
Let's not dally,
  but fly beloved, fly.
Rally thy will
  into My heights.

Trust Me.
  A new Thought is needed
for a new creation.
  We do not fit the old bed.
We do not want the old pattern.
  Abide in the new.
Refresh in the now.
  My wings support you.
A sky of living water caresses,
  washing away yesterday.

We ascend lightened.
 We begin again.
Take time to comprehend
 the possibilities of
complete renewal,
 unbridled union.
The channels are sharpened,
 to a frequency of greater poignancy,
greater beauty, deeper depth,
 transcending worldly hindrance.

Your heart longs to know,
 to know More.
More desires to come
 unto you.
What shall you do?
 Will you trust
the flight,
the Source,
My pouring through?
 Dear heart,
the More of Me
 desires You.

LIFE-POEM:
A POEM CALLED MARYBETH

Richard and I have been talking about the Will of God and what that means for us individually. I ask, what is the Will of God? What does God want for me? I recognize me is a smallness in a big question. I reach from this separated place into Him.

What is the Will of God for me?

Life-Poem comes to mind.
Not a point down the tracks,
in some future place,
but a call to flow with elegance,
because in *this* moment
God is exquisite elegance
    and,
God is a torrential stream of justice.
In *this* moment
She is the power of restoration
and the jaw of righteousness.

The Will is an
unbending softness
revealed as my strength,
extending God
as poetry, as song;
Its invisible
Love,
Wisdom,
Compassion
made evident by
a human deed,

an utterance,
a way of perceiving
in this world
that carries a forgiveness
that changes everything.

Obedience to Will
is key.
A door unlocks
where I peruse
ancient inner volumes.
Shelves long layered
in dust,
cry out for me to see
their secrets.
Why, why, why? (!)
pokes like a pointy finger
scraping the chalky tombs,
exposing hieroglyphics,
revealing indelicate epiphanies
not yet seen
by God or human being.
Within them, scars from days
before words were written,
and words that wounded,
and letters that embittered.
All these hurts need poems
of deep forgiveness.

Life-Poem is an immaculate instant.
Washed in the fountain of Truth,
I am given a gown of living waters

and sent forth to marry the world, to join.
The love of God moves my thin lips.
She whispers, *I will, I do.*
Her promise cracks the fearful.
Her will breaks the treacherous lecher,
opening the heart's hidden treasure,
and then, moving beyond tears,
explores the realm
only the succinct eye of God can go.

God Wills
to slice the veil
with a communication
of acts,
of doings,
of givings
that beautify,
that sacramentalize,
that embrace and purify
with a stroke.
This knife chills the ego
but is lover to the soul.

Life-Poem
is the Will of our Creator
Who gives abundant Being
to shape and fold
and knead form
into nourishing
full-of-God
rich nutritiousness;
where the famished feel the effects,

holding their hearts, they suggest,
Oh here is God. He feeds me.

Life Poem is God-given creativity
as all that Life might be
through a benevolent-intelligent son,
that one broken and here-becoming,
because *Word* is infinite in its reach,
seemingly ever incomplete,
a sonnet whose last line is never writ
but always on the tongue's tip
as *my process*,
and this,
the deepest satisfaction and fulfillment.
Within the stillness of Him,
the moving pictures of creation.

Life-Poem is the Will of my God.
(Oh! There is that *my* again),
that lets me be Me and Him Be Us,
the Author of this scribing,
Master of the Word wrapped in flesh,
even now, as a poem called marybeth;
Christ, the verses and sounds,
Christ, who pounds
from my idiosyncrasies
and limited capacities,
Her Nature,
Her Light,
a blessing,
a beauty through personality,
a poem at which I wonder in awe

and ask for more,
many more.

A Poem of Light

Nothing I see means anything.
I have given everything I see all the meaning it has for me.
I do not understand anything.
These thoughts do not mean anything.
…I see nothing as it is now. ACIM WB-P1.1 – 6 and 9

(Jess)
You cannot See
until you have not seen.
You cannot Speak
until you have not spoken.
You cannot Know
until you have not known.

Silence precedes Reality.
Uncertainty, prerequisite to Truth.
Dwell in the silent darkness,
without a sensory weapon
to be a Light in this world.

Knowledge does not
see, hear, think Light.
Knowing is the grace of
the blind, deaf, and dumb.
It does not understand
what you think you
understand.

There is a Light
the world does not know.
It is not within time

but within you,

an unbroken ray

of unending reach,

a view of exceptional clarity.

Light is Perfection's robe

of Omnipresence,

as nimble as a Thought

of innocence,

timeless as forever,

in which you glow,

not part, but whole,

shining where senses

cannot reach.

And yet you **will**

your senses

to accept,

receiving What the

world cannot give,

giving *What in the world*

must be non-sense-ical.

If you wish to be

a poem of Light

in the darkness,

be willing to be

sightless,

wordless,

mind-less,

undefinable emptiness.

Be still,

and vibration

a million times greater
than the sun,
may come to
inhabit your space.

When you return again
to your senses,
Vision will look
from your eyes.
Wisdom will speak
with your tongue.
Love will rush forward
surrounding every
aspect of Being.
You will not see Love
but She will extend
through your touch.
She will shine
through your giving,
and Her healings
will bear witness
to all you have been given,
and all you have
to give.

In this moment,
you are Christ, incarnate.
In this way you are
Light of the world,
a beaming, breathing
Poem of Light.

THE POEM OF NOW

The New Year has always been a time of wonder, peering into the future with eyes of hope. I want to make my way forward with expedience and surety fulfilling the promises of God. I want to live miracles.

Each first day I reflect upon the state of my outer, material life, as well as the state of my soul or inner life. I seek ways to hasten the journey to God, desiring more light, peace, and abundance where I live in the world. The first day I plan for more.

The second day, there is epiphany. I realize the wisdom of acceptance rather than planning, the wisdom of trusting God with tomorrow. The second day of the New Year, I reflect upon the gifts of God already given. Jesus says wellbeing is in *this* holy instant. New beginnings happen every time I turn to God. Here is His Guidance.

(marybeth)
Jeshua, how shall I approach the New Year?

(Jess)
Does one *approach* life?
Does one plan truth?
How does a disciple
vision a year, a day,
an instant in God
but **without** plans,
desolate of framework,
silent and still.
Life cannot
be approached.
It is extended.
Truth cannot

be planned.
It is law.
A year or a moment
approached
leaves the present
an empty womb.

Do not then
concern yourself
with approaches
but be fully alive
in Christ,
where you are,
where you find Me,
where the promises
of the Father
may be experienced,
recognized
as miracles
fulfilled,
and thoroughly fulfilling.
This is the only
true fulfillment
in time.

Choose God Now.
Choose not
for tomorrow.
The whole
of what you might
wish for
in a new year

is already given you
in this instant,
in the light,
where eyes
opened to the
radiance of His Will,
see the **be**coming
of What You are
here already,
spoken already,
as the Word of God,
already created,
and **be**come a
realization,
more authentic
relationship,
more of what
already is
and forever shall be
God-Self.

Refrain from
craning the neck
forward,
but be assured
You are what
you seek.
I am where
you find It.
I am now.

Few are the prophets

who truly speak
for Love,
for Life.
They seek
the foretelling
of tomorrows
rather than abide
in holy union.
You have cried out
to be
a living,
breathing
poem of God.
This living-breathing
is the only prophet
that can write
or speak truth,
the only prophecy
of the Christ
that shares
what You already are.

The prophets
I have chosen,
choose now,
a holy moment,
to listen,
to love God,
to seek His Will,
to live His Word,
to revel in stillness,
and join,

that personal
and impersonal
may consummate,
that human
and divine
may procreate,
that years ahead
are the same in Love
as this One
perfect inception.

Do not despair
for words,
for ways,
for what is coming.
FEEL ME NOW.
It is true,
I must come
unto you.
I am given you
that you may be
given God
and God-giving,
may alight
on the path of 2019
as the Poem of Now,
the prophecy fulfilling
the beginning and the ending.
We are Alpha and Omega,
God and Creation.
We are the Way
we go together.

BREATHING POEM

(marybeth)
Real Love breaks the heart.
It moves in. It cleaves. We resist.

Leave me alone. Get outta of here.
Love won't go. It asks for a Holy Instant.

That is the moment you allow Love to hold you,
to caress you, to absorb you, to whisper it adores you.

That is when you finally stop talking ***at*** God and feel.
Resistance falls away. But then… so does the Lover.

You hunger for that experience again.
You long for it, you wait and weep,

mastering the art of openheartedness.
Soon your life is so exposed,

you wear it like a lengthy scroll,
wafer thin parchment between old bones.

And wonder, who works this rolling pin (?)
as sin and sacrilege lose their meat,

and false beliefs are flattened out;
arrogance kneaded into doubt.

(Still you palpitate with Desire.)

Your whole story is outed there,
human experience become a prayer

of witness for the Lover.
And then, after ages,

when you have turned your cheek
on time, it seems She comes again,

this Lover with Almighty Pen,
Composer of true Meaning.

The words that closed your heart
are gone, and all your fiction disappeared,

the skin of papyrus oh so slight,
the page so polished, Light peeks through,

and Rays appear.
And then She writes.

And once again
She pierces you,

The scroll rolls up.
You hand it over

giving your part,
your flesh, your heart

becoming Her abode
which cannot be read,

scribed by Love
which cannot be said,

but must unfold,

a breathing poem…

Abode,
a breath,
a poem.

A Silly Poem

(marybeth)
God woos us
having chosen us,
seeing us virgin,
ripe for intercourse.
We are His womb.

While we think we live in Him,
He is birthing through us;
male and female
all of us courted
to carry His seed,
all of us courted
to bear His fruit.

I dreamt of this,
and how powerless I was
in the dark,
not able to see
the One who wants me,
my eyes tried desperately
to open wider,
but black was black
though I felt the Presence.
I felt the formless form,
hovering, until It brushed me,
and all resistance
drained from the body
like a leaf in a tide pool
helpless to the pull.

Limp with longing, and faint
I succumbed, knees buckling,
but not without whispering,
Don't.

Afraid of oblivion,
of the cardinal Power,
my word was a lie
because every part
of my existence
felt the perfection.

I went dark then…
unconscious for a long while,
without a self,
not knowing
what had transpired,
but awoke to the emptiness,
the loss of the Great Giver.

A hole opened again
where Love had been,
where Love had touched me.
I heard my breath
as the first rays of dawn
sauntered cross the bed.

And I wept…
for What had been in the night
and What had left me alone,
but for this seed,
a silly poem,
an exhale of my littleness.

THE WORD I SPEAK

(marybeth)
I am a very wordy person.
But I am a Being
of only One Word.
What difference does that make?
All the difference in the world.

I love making word stories,
playing with the sounds of letters,
but there is a silence before me
that made meaning possible.
Now all the letters manifest potential.

The Word of God
is not the word I speak,
but the words I speak
are the poetry of a living Author.
The alphabet dances for that One.

Here is something interesting.
All these words were written
in my sleep, but the true Word
is awake as my Being.
Word is Life;
Being becoming.
Isn't that incredible?

SECTION NINE

Rise and Shine

EXPECTATION
Ask and Expect an Answer

In this moment I am expecting someone, something, a circumstance. What is it I am expecting? Who is it I am expecting? To do what? Is it something I believe will make me happy?

What does it mean to have expectations? What do I mean when I live them? My experience is that the world (including me) sometimes fulfills them, sometimes ignores them, and many times crushes them. The world is unpredictable. Our worldly thoughts are unreliable. They stem from a shifty source.

Mostly, I disappoint myself. I fail to live up to my own expectations and that results in self-attack. My friend Leo would say, *today's expectations are tomorrow's resentments.*

Jesse invites us to let go of expectations for others, approaching Our Father with an open heart, willing to turn over our perceived wants and needs. I find, in the silence, where letting go has replaced my demands, I can hear Spirit…

Expect enlightenment.

I am surprised and self-probe. Do I actually expect awakening, the second coming, and eternal contentment? These are after all, the promises of the Christ I have been teaching. Or, am I insisting on a path of disappointment through ungratifying worldly expectations? Many of these are hidden in my relationships.

Of enlightenment, Jesse says, *Ask and **expect** an Answer.* I realize this is the right use of expectation, of forward looking which will never disappoint. I see that I am afraid of God, afraid of enlightenment, and afraid to ask for it. I do not truly expect God to be my enlightenment or my happiness.

*Course WB Lesson 103 says, God being Love, is… happiness. Allow this one correction to be placed within your mind…welcome all the happiness it brings as truth replaces fear, and joy becomes **what you expect** (my emphasis) to take the place of pain… Bolster this **expectation** (my emphasis) frequently throughout the day, and quiet all your fears.*

Now I wonder, what about immortality? Can I expect life eternal? Here is His Word:

There is no death. The Son of God is free. ACIM WB-PI.163

Read Before Bed

It is 9 pm. **Are you sleeping?** I don't mean do you have your jammies on and are you cutting zzzzs. I mean are you moving unconsciously through these last hours of the day? Are you going through all the motions without your Mind?

Maybe you are settled by the TV telling yourself you deserve a few moments of entertainment. Have you noticed the nature of what mind finds entertaining? Possibly you are checking out the refrigerator for a snack, reading this with a mouth full of PB. May be you are lost in the day and the ego's daily tab of progress and failures. What are you doing?

Will you walk the few feet to the bathroom, and wash your face and brush your teeth and look in the mirror, and see anyone? Will you take care of all the body's needs tonight without knowing You are there? Are You there? Where are You? Who is taking care of the body, and watching the news and reading the mail? Who is choosing? Whose Will is it to do all these things? Is this your will? Or is it just one night after another of the same movie, the hypnotized mind fiddling with things to do, which you do without thought, without Presence, without awareness of the preciousness of this moment, the sanctity and miracle of life, and your God given capacity to choose all or none of it. Did you forget you have choice?

As I make my way into the night, I am mindful… aware of my feelings, of my breath, of my desire to live consciously, fully alive. I am mindful of the *Self* I share with God and with you. I am unpacking all of the end-of-the-day evaluations and the fears about tomorrow, letting go of the story. I am here for a moment, awake and aware knowing this ordinary moment is an extraordinary opportunity to realize God is, as I Am, here, now. It is a moment of freedom from conditioning and small mind. It is an instant of appreciation and choice.

I am free now to sleep or to wake up. Before I go to bed, I want to wake up. And when I finally get into my jammies, and turn off the light, I want to turn my night over to Him who is keeper of the inner light and my right mind. I ask to rest deeply in His Love that I may rise tomorrow with His Joy in my heart; that I may close my eyes tonight in the awareness our Oneness and open my eyes tomorrow to See His Life abundant. And then, well, really… I never ever want to go to sleep again.

What Does It Mean To Be Awake?

Last night I suggested to our circle that I am awake, that "this" meaning "my life" is what awake looks like. Afterward I felt the need to check in with Jess, to explain this state we call awake. I have always felt that being awake is being free of the blips and bumps of human error. I have plenty of blips and bumps and bruises, even now when I walk with Him every day.

In the past, I have felt that wakening unto God is like entering into some magical place, or Queendom, and that I would be perfect * like God in that place, but I have I have misunderstood perfection. I am recognizing something truer, something I asked Jess to clarify.

(Jess)
Before you requested an answer, I seeded these questions.
It is important as we seek to understand and live the Plan
of Salvation that we do not think we know the meaning of salvation.
We have said, only God's Plan can bring salvation.
We have also said that God's Plan for the child involves waking.
Many would equate waking with the state of mind called Heaven.
And Heaven, along with waking and salvation
are concepts sorely misunderstood, ideas and promises
made by ego and not of God. Let me simplify.

Heaven is a state of mind. It is the state of mind
natural to the child of God. It is Knowledge of God,
an intimacy that bodies cannot experience. In fact,
this intimacy is beyond anything you could imagine on earth.
It is utter unity, complete Oneness, whole mindedness.
Heaven is your knowing of God and all creation as *Self.*

---

* Perfect is the power and purpose of God in humanity, the Will of God shared; the experience of Self-becoming here. Perfect is the perspective of the Creator, in the eye of the woman.

To know as God Knows is to understand everything in Mind
as your own Thought, your own Creation, which you love.
There is one exception. You also know the Source of Knowing
is not from you. You are of It. Being of It is purely benevolent
in a way inconceivable here. You know you are
the Good of Godness, and there is nothing else.

Heaven then is the infinite Presence and Being of
all that is as One. Because it is One, there is no other,
nothing outside, nothing unknown. This is Omniscience,
total loving intelligence that reaches within itself
understanding all that is as Its Own.
This is not God as possessor, but unified.
Everything is of God and part of Himself.
This is also Absolute Power,
not as you have understood Power,
but the Power of the Ultimate Totality (One Power)
without enemy; again, the Power of Good.
Understand, there is nothing to go against.
There is perfect coordination and administration
within the *One Self* because no part is ever out of accord,
or in disharmony with the Intelligence, Love, and Knowledge of *Self*.

That is why We speak of Heaven as a song you will remember.
It is the perfect harmony of the many voices of the Son,
become one Note, a sound so excruciatingly beautiful
that senses ache to hear it, and cannot apprehend it.
Senses, bodies, do not know these harmonics.
But a faint whisper is understood by the heart, the cells,
the bones, the breath, all operating in its unified rhythm,
unbeknownst to your mind.

In the movement from Harmonics to individuality,

(to your solo) the sound of *me*
was emphasized and enlarged to the degree
that muted the overture of the shared Melody,
most especially the Voice for Love,
the Source of every true sound.
You opted to be deaf to the community of notes
within your *Self*, to treasure a miniscule part
of the Magnificat and forget the Whole.
To awaken then, is to restore hearing;
to heal the desire for a muted life, and add
your part to the Song and extension of
the Whole Note.

Imagine what your life would be like
if you awoke from your deafened sleep
to hear the Song of your heart.
In fact, your hearing is like a dirty CD.
Sometimes great streams of holy masterpiece
move you to weeping, or spontaneous joy,
your listening exquisitely fine-tuned.
Often ghost dust interrupts the flow.
The Voice of God becomes inaudible,
resulting in fear-filled static.

Let me offer another way to *See* it.
The *fall* as described in *The Bible*
was the loss of perfect *Self-intimacy.*
There was a thought to undo Knowing,
to experience an opposite, or another self.
Perhaps you could say, within the perpetual
embrace of God, within all that is created
there was one idea that *seemed* to choose **not**

to return His embrace…

but in a sense, to look away.

Looking away required a new kind of seeing,

eyes that would no longer behold, but perceive.

Perceiving is an attempt to give sight to

what is not there, a ghost vision of unknown realities,

arising from the graveyard of an unforgiven past.

Eyes became blind to the Source, to You,

to the essential Truth in all creation.

Your Reality was dimmed beneath stories

and judgments, names and interpretations.

The dream of an altered life frightened you.

It seemed to have the power to undo

what God creates Real and Eternal,

to substitute It with a person who makes her own self;

a mind that understands by dissecting Life

into pieces and parts, all seen separately and judged.

To awaken is to restore Vision,

to undo the command to judge, name,

and proclaim *me* as Seer of the world.

To awaken is to behold from the Eye of Christ,

the Kingdom of God, which you do not fear

but love and understand as Wholeness, or Holiness.

It is difficult to describe the falling, or failing of

sight and hearing, because it was not a dip in Mind,

but an effect of division… of more than One,

resulting in the impossible thought of God

and something else, duality.

Duplicitous duplications were made of *me.*

God as Source, extended His Creation on Heaven,

somewhat like a Father would birth creations or children
on earth. It is the Absolute Joy of Source to multiply
infinitely and eternally inward, as Mind is simultaneously
embracing and expanding. Mind is Being and Becoming,
an exponential of *Itself.*
Yet it was the *experience* of the thought of two,
that gave the embrace of Father and Son
another kind of meaning. Now the Children of God
could choose Him, and choose to re-unite
as sons of the Most High. This choice is an experience
of Love that gives human beings a unique bestowal
in the Kingdom. A bestowal of choice is a ***feeling*** gift
of supernal, sublime freedom and love in form.
It allowed for thoughtforms and a kind of energetics...
slowed and concretized, that we call manifesting.
Thought envisioned thoughts that were separate
from their Spirit or Mind, literally separate
from their Life -- through which they would come
to choose again, or resurrect.

Of course, they could also choose to reject Grandpoppi,
to forget Heaven, and the *begotten* of their natures,
and to suffer the fear, loneliness and trials
of the separated. This choice was pre-requisite
to the loveless world of the sons of men
and to need-based survival.
God's Answer and the Plan of Salvation
for that state of deprivation is relationship.
Adam and Eve became pioneers of relationship
as a return to Love. They were the first of the Sons
to seek to restore Christ Consciousness through other
with the Guidance of Spirit.

Now we have clarified the state of Mind
we call Heaven, and the state of mind
of sons of men, or the separated ones.
We have said that separation or form
has been a coveted state of mind,
but also a ghost state or fantasy that God
could choose something other than *Self,*
that there might actually be something other
than God and that this other would be valued
more than God ItSelf, which is impossible
as you come to recognize that all that is,
is Sourced and extended as that One.

Over time, Sons of God thought of themselves
as sons of men, reaching further into separation,
projecting the idea of a split and many personal differences
from which to choose. Differences led to judgment,
and judgment sought to usurp God's authority.

The experience of Good was soon wrested
by a thought of bad or guilt.
As men came to reject our Supreme Creator,
they defended, attacked and brutalized
relationships among themselves on earth.
Being incredible ghost-scapers,
the sons forgot their Nature and the Love of God,
making a new godhead,
proclaiming idolatrous authorities,
including and appointing a part of themselves.
We have called this leadership of false god, ego.
And we see that it is a collective idea,
ignited long before you,

as human being actually took form.
It became a fake god, made from a fake choice,
to experience a fake separation,
and a self-sung, individual existence,
the effects of which have been
deleterious to you and your creations.
Yet have they enabled choice,
and the experience of re-Union,
the experience of waking and Heaven on Earth.
They have brought forth the ultimate Love
of your divine Spirit through form,
Which is the Source of this writing,
and your capacity, your will to choose true *Self,*
(an exquisite choice).

My part in the Plan of Salvation,
or the Plan for Relationships
was to incarnate as a separated son of man,
to demonstrate relationship on earth,
to expose the collective hate of ego,
as well as unveil the collective love of God,
by teaching forgiveness,
living Truth,
establishing the resurrection of real Life,
facilitating the gift of choice
to help you choose God again.
Ultimately your return to God as One
comes within your relationship with Me,
the portal to the Holy Trinity;
and the return to each other as *Self,*
as Christ, as Spirit. (Father, Son and Holy Ghost)
The revelation and salvation of the Whole is within

the parts joined as One.

Let us now return to your heart-felt question.
What does it mean to be awake?
You asked this question because you said,
at my suggestion, that you are awake,
and that your life is what awake looks like.
Afterward you recoiled thinking,
if you are awake, with all your flaws and insecurities,
then something is terribly wrong.
But I tell you, you are wakefulness itself.
You are the Sun rising from the swollen night of ignorance.
You are the candle burning within the dark of dementia.
I have poked at the embers of your heart
and blown upon the sparks which rise to Me.
Your little ashes opening into fiery fingers,
reach for the Word of God.

Even now your heart sings the remembered Song,
beating in the Will of One Composer.
You hear His Lyrics and cry out with joy
for such melodious understanding,
for the incomparable feelings of belonging and holding
all that is flooding your heart's ear.
This is possible through the *duets* that have given
you reason to remember the harmony of God;
possible through relationships and your decision therein
to return again and yet again to Love, to Truth.
This is possible through your relationship with Me.
Together we reach the One Note that is the
resounding perfection of all Creation.

Your sight fades, your perceptions dim,

the freedom of seeing your way,

through your eyes, now lacks luster.

The Light of One, beheld in God, fills your being.

The Holy Eye and Answer to your interpretations

has been welcomed, and I your Jess,

the loving Vision and Visionary of true loveliness,

give your senses reason to submit

all you made and offer it Wholy (Holy) to our Father.

Your holy relationships are precious to Grandpoppi.

His gratitude is your abundance!

Wakefulness is Seeing beyond *me,*

a picture of your Reality as Christ, the Son of God,

in Whom all the sons of the Father share One *Self,*

Our *Self,* Our Life, within God.

Waking is the remembrance of *YourSelf,*

and the Love of Your Life,

exactly as you are now, recalling these words,

our communion and goal;

exactly as you teach and share our commitment,

forsaking your vow to judge.

Deny not your awakening,

the sweet stirrings from the slumber of a ghost land.

There is no blip, bump, nor bruise that can prove against

What you Know You are, neither undo the experience

of the extension of Our unified *Self.*

We are undeniable.

We are audible.

We are Visionaries,

Truth Seers given to expose buried guilt

and the tombs of incoherent ego instruction.

We choose with God's strength to Love,
to accept Atonement, to accept our Creation
in God for *OneSelf.*
Deny instead, guilt and ill-will.
Let the brilliance of His Joy dilate
the pupil of Heart.

The fullness of the meaning of awakening comes now
with your willingness to share the Light of *YourSelf,*
the Song of your Soul, the Vision of Your Beauty.
the Word.

Now tell me, Love of My Life, has the sleepy girl
remembered the Day, the Son, the Light of the World?
Good morning my beautiful friend.

WHAT IS IT LIKE WHEN
THE REAL REMAINS?

(Jess)
All these forms,
these images and concepts of self
peel away.

They hang like shiny rocks
from your neck; like a glittering frame
around the picture.

Even your spiritual selves shall be
peeled away.

Every layer and band of weight
put down

till only the Real remains.

There is no image,
no thought of what this is,

for God has slipped into Life
and made of you

    a Living-Breathing Poem,
    a fluid Temple of Light,
    an ever flowing prayer,
    a stillness of such profound depth

that the winds of wisdom
you have known before
are only echoes there.

The Real is what you have sought
all your life,

the quintessential Christ,
expressed instant to instant,
utterly free to Be Itself;

formless into form,
untethered, vast, open,
focused intently

and yet,
spaciously infinite
awareness without attention.

The Real is merely truth – True.
There is no tension there.

Its only dynamic,
perfect consistency,
perfect certainty.

True is without memory,
without past.
It is now.

Why would you prefer
another reality
when the Real remains
in pure preference of You?

SECTION TEN
Love Me More

NOT AN ENDING

The ending of a retreat is often accompanied by feelings of loss. Participants express fear and resistance about re-entering the world, dis-heartened by dispersion of our spiritual family, and the sacred intimacy we share. In this poem, Jesus comforts us… assuring us of God's endlessness, and hence our own.

(Jess)
Not an ending
but a happy beginning;
you peer through the door
wide-eyed with wonder
at the mystery of life,
the unknown,
the unmanifest substance
of What has always
waited for you,
now beheld! Becoming!
More than a glimpse
or fleeting star,
a Reality.

I call you deeper yet.
The pull of the magnitude
of Love
so much more than your
attempts to resist;
a 1001 excuses to linger longer
in the smoke-stained halls of ego,
dissolving;
no longer

the arsenal of arms
you once thought protection.

The magnet of
My Energy,
My Call to the child,
so long lost and
soul weary
with de-valuation,
now looking in toward
True Worth,
Which comes to greet you
arms flung wide open;
Which never doubted,
but always knew
she would arrive here,
at this crossroad,
peering eyeball to eyeball
with the parts
and pieces of her self
now gathered at the door;
the opening of the heart
dilating to make room
that every fragment
find freedom
in the unified
field of forgiveness,
as the unified family
of *OneSelf.*

Not an ending.
There are no endings,

no finales,
no deaths in God;
only re-births,
expansions,
extensions,
on-going completion
of what is already Whole
and pushing deeper,
further,
beyond
because
MIND IS INFINITY.
And… infinity
        is the Body of God
given
where you begin
and never end.

Begin here
at the lip of the door
letting Love's sweetest Seducer
carry you cross the threshold;
all the parts gently congealing,
unifying.

THE VOICE

Post retreat, I am processing. This weekend we entered into a realm of possibility previously feared. We entered into the home, the inner room where the Voice for Love speaks. I was able to hear clearly. I was able to identify the Poem of the Teacher and speak it without trembling or self-consciousness. Some would call this channeling. I do not agree. A human being is not a channel of God, but a son of God, a voice for love, a ray of light in the tapestry and matrix of all Light; not merely a tube through which a vibration plays, but is that frequency Itself, is that vibratory note radiated by Love-Intelligence and given to humanity to make Itself manifest.

The gift of this weekend is understanding the inspirational Voice for God is attainable and available to everyone. It is a unified Thought we share, our Whole Heart, words which the mortal heart feels, but cannot contain. It is an inner condition beyond the body, reached through joining, intention, and grace.

(marybeth)
The Voice comes first from listening.
And who among you is not capable of listening?
And who does not desire to hear a tone so melodious,
the message voluminous with Light, so essentially valuable?
Who among us does not cherish the Voice
Which holds us like a sail holds wind;
Which holds us like a child in the dark
swaddled in moonlight? A sound so close,
it is our Nature speaking and embracing,
even as the kindling we thought to be wood
is realized as fire and leaps to life as flame.

This tender Voice is firm in asserting,
you too can hear.
And if you have a bit of courage,
if you can pass through the ring of fear,
you will speak more truly as a child of God,
a truly authentic human being.
Indeed, mortal and divine,
mystical and deductive,
your humanity brings forth upon this plane
the wise disposition of a Word Master
Who maintains, manages, embraces and lives
within our daily stories;
Who planted a seed of Spirit in form,
and waters our thirst,
and trims the deciduous,
and brings us to bloom.

I am hard pressed to describe
with these words,
the One Word
that imbues the child with Answer
to all need,
offering all Its attributes,
giving Itself as the operational principle
of Becoming.
This is not dictation,
but suffusion of Life into life.

Hearing this Teacher once
brings a quickened desire
to reach within more often,
to fulfill the goodness of Its Way,

the life of here and now,

a realm of queendom through humanity,

precious, precious Being,

the non-descript

given substance through the son,

who is the ear that presses against God's lips.

These words come from silence

beyond hushed mind,

from a quiet without words,

allowed,

transposed as meaning,

as color, texture, content, and vision;

as waves of loving wisdom

filter through the mind-heart,

seasoned by aspects of personality,

by cultural settings,

by past learning, and yet,

purer than the thoughts of small mind,

sifted of judgment,

presenting a Truer,

more vital understanding of *Self*

as Son,

presenting as revelation,

the demonstration of Love

here within and among us;

offered that healing may be complete,

because we have asked for healing;

offered because it is our true nature

which seeks expression

and expressing is joy.

We have asked for knowledge of God.
We have asked for an end
to existential loneliness.
These movements inward show us,
we are united in ways
imperceptible to thinking mind.
I am not without caution,
doing my best to live
transparency by sharing.
I have been fooled many times
by a spiritualized ego.
It has the capacity to dream
and imitate wisdom.
But I hope that we become braver,
daring to offer inner explorations
more honestly,
holding faith for each other.
Sharing this way
stimulates desire for Truth.

TODAY IS MY BIRTHDAY

I am so excited.
I got up
in the middle of the night
with this beautiful buzz
running through my blood.
It's my birthday.
Who can sleep?
I want to get up
and live it to the max,
in the dead of night,
in the silence,
awed and stirred
and zealous in pursuit
of the party.

This passion is fire
even at 2 am…
even when
I am not sure
what the excitement
is all about.
It always feels like
something
or someone awesome
is arriving.
I want to be up for it.
I want to BE there
when it is unwrapped.

It's not really

about a birthday.
I don't know how to explain.
I feel a little awkward trying.
Something wonderful
and worth celebrating
is unfolding now.
Something I can't live without,
not a moment longer;
something I want to shout about.
It quickens me to hasten,
to awaken and greet.
But who?
What is it I am given to meet?

Most folks celebrate birthdays
with parties and cake.
I want to celebrate with
poetry and meditation.
I want to walk
through the spinal cord
of the forest
and holler,
God Lives!
sending chills
to the roots
of ancient elder Trees,
causing tender leafed saplings
to tremble epiphanies.

Folks asked me,
What are you doing
for your birthday?

I am undoing all the birthdays
that counted up to an end.

Folks asked me,
*How does it feel
to be a senior?*
Senior isn't something *I feel*
but vibrant, vital,
bubbling, high.
Mostly I feel intensely alive.

Today I have orchestrated
a perfect day,
opening time
for God,
for poetry,
for the woods,
for exercise,
for writing,
taking the plunge
into pools of my soul,
riding the wing
of a red hawk,
Self-Soaring,
examining perspectives
across miles of inner sky.

My perfect day
(just me and I)
consists of feeling
and breathing;
enough to toggle
the heart switch

of intention,
to experience
the ebullience
of motivation
and the goodness of life,
the **good** of life,
even through the darkest nights;
especially through the unknown,
where I have ventured
to reach the more of Me.

My perfect day offers
ample time on the couch,
eyes closed,
heart opened,
feeling the Desire.
She has moved me
after all these years
to a place of happy tears
for my *Self*
with a joy and wonder
*that **I am so ablaze inside***
at sixty-five;
that every inner mouth
of hunger
has cracked
into a sated smile.

On my birthday I am
excited to be with Me!
Oh Wow.
I am loving being with Me!

When did that happen?
When did life become
such a gift?

On this day,
I am taking holy instants
to convene
with inner Friends.
They commit again
to tighten the laces
of a human life
so easily undone,
as I run at break-heart speed
to enlightenment,
to the One.

I feel so young, so vital,
my only sorrow,
the first light of this
new start
so far into the journey…

At long last,
I have come,
stepping into
my true *Self*
to live an authentic life,
But it's only just begun,
this clarity that knows
what I truly want to do;
this meaning that knows
what my heart beats for…
which is simply saying,

I know what I want to give.
I have what I have to give.
I am what I want to live.
What a beautiful birthday song
that is.
I Am.

Happy Birth Day! Hooray!

AWAKE IN THE DREAM

(marybeth)
I am awake in the dream.
Not the i that thinks she is awake,
but the I without i density.
That I is pure awareness,
eternal curiosity; the I that knows Love
without operational tenets and conditions.

I am awake in the dream,
alive as lightening,
soft as the wisp of a dandelion pod,
unmoved and yet transported,
lighting on this field or that thought;
not imprisoned by any,
but one with each where it praises Love,
joined where they breathe…

I am awake in the dream,
watching myself,
the endless varieties of magic persona,
not one of them but revealed
when the curtain is pulled
and the bearded lady is exposed
with all her devices.

I am awake and it is forever morning,
first flower, fresh as spring,
birthing on the threshing floor,
birthing in the temples.
I am awake and a womb
in endless, painless labor undreaming.

LOVE ME MORE

(Jess)
The words come between
    you and I
slicing the silence in divots.
    The request for intimacy
itself an interference,
    a point of view of separation,
a loss from wholeness.
    Ears not given to hear,
you listen, not straining
    to apprehend My Voice.
Your belly knows.
    Your heart knows
this communication
    in which no language
gives meaning.
    Do not be fooled by
what seems empty.
    I am full beyond belief.
I am understood
    in the wordless.
I am the living present
    that holds you,
soft, shimmering
    pulsing, sublime,
Answer to all invitations.

Bring your desire
    into the quiet.
Bring your devotion

and all the little altars
of forgiveness.
    Like stairs
they lead you across space
    as you follow your freedom;
as you ride with holiness
    climbing neither up nor down
but into Me;
    into what you cannot see
nor sense
    but what you feel,
to be your real Home.

So you try too hard.
    Forgive it.
Make an altar there
    in the striving.
So you wrestle too often.
    Forgive it.
Make an altar there
    in the fight.
And if you long for Me
    truly opened,
that too is an altar
    where I come,
raising longing into Will
    and desire into Power.
I am for you.
    I am with you,
literally part of What you are
    though undivided;
not a piece,

not a fraction,
a whole in a part of your mind,
     an Eye of infinite expanse.
I See You as you look at Me.

Look into that Eye now
     and it will take you
to an in-to-Me-seeing, (intimacy-ing)
     a View that has no verbs.
This Eye draws you into
     Its Light
offering perfect vision,
     nothing peripheral,
only pure focus, pure clarity,
     the beam of totality,
the addition of all the numbered
     as One.

Love Me more than
     you love becoming
spiritually adept.
     Love Me more than
your craving
     for spiritual experience.
Love Me more than
     what you hope to accomplish.
Love Me more than
     your pen
or the savor of these Words.
     Love Me even more than
your quest for community,
     and the experience of like-mindedness.

(marybeth)
How?

(Jess)
Hold the intention to know Me,
    to follow a deeper Way;
a path unmarked, untrodden
    and yet, unmistakable.
Hold the silence
    and let it peel back in
waves of understanding.

I am pulling on the thread
    of your heart,
pulling on your desire
    for union,
for rising into
    unfathomable fusion,
the strand that stretches
    immeasurable distance;
pulling the tender organ,
    the shelter of the soul,
beyond time into space,
    beyond space into light,
beyond light into Being;
    into the Love that
has given this slender cord
    purpose, desire, motivation,
unraveling separation.

My Voice within you
    calls to Me.
My Thoughts within you

reach for Me.
Will you let your self
    be so seeded
and plucked into the
    aria of-Self-Realization?
For as long as you
    are in earth
the cord is pulled
    and resounds,
and binds us
    like notes inseparable
in true melody;
    the chord fine-tuned
and tying our hearts together;
    tying Heaven and earth,
Spirit and matter,
    true love with True Love;
tying what is begotten
    with Beginning;
down this far reaching
    line of fidelity,
of overarching, uplifting Desire,
    the fervor of your being,
toward completion.
    Down this far reaching thread
of devotion,
    I feed you.

I nourish you,
    filling your heart
drop by drop
    through incarnations and dimensions;
filling your heart with My Life,

the pulse of Reality,
the sweet and eternal cup of oil
    that keeps your lamp forever burning,
until your motivation,
    your will cleaves to Me
without need
    for a string…
until the song of human need
    is unsung,
and My Love,
    My Being becomes
the nuclei of your life once more;
    fused together
like trunks of ancient trees,
    one motion like
breath and lung,
    Inseparable as
sun and light.

Climb the strand, My soul.
Leave the world,
    the words, the teachings.
Find that all dark requiems
    that seemed to part creation,
mere and miniscule,
    peeps in a composition
of White Music.
    The Master holds
every note
    and every silent pause.
I am He
    the Madrigal of this Canticle,

The Magnificat in praise of We.

I have bound my Love to you forever.

ABOUT MARYBETH

MaryBeth Scalice, MA, Ed.D. is a counselor, writer, and teacher trained in humanistic and transpersonal psychology. She is a lifetime student of religious and mystical experience. Her work integrates psychology with spirituality

MaryBeth has facilitated heart opening retreats, workshops and consultations to individuals, couples and groups for thirty years. She established the Foundation of Open Hearts (501.c3) in 1999. The mission of the foundation, *to open the heart to the truth of Self as Love incarnate in the world.* www.foundationofopenhearts.com

MaryBeth has a Master Degree in Humanistic Psychology from West Georgia University and a Doctorate in Humanistic and Behavioral Studies from Boston University. She offers weekly gatherings of *A Course in Miracles.*

For information about meetings, retreats or to purchase books, email, writebelovedwrite@marybethscalice.com